ONE HUNDRED AND FIFTY SHARDS OF LIGHT

Michael Levitton

**Grosvenor House
Publishing Limited**

The right of Michael Levitton to be identified as the author of this
work has been asserted by him in accordance with Section 78
of the Copyright, Designs and Patents Act 1988

The book cover picture is copyright to Inmagine Corp LLC

This book is published by
Grosvenor House Publishing Ltd
28-30 High Street, Guildford, Surrey, GU1 3EL.
www.grosvenorhousepublishing.co.uk

A CIP record for this book
is available from the British Library

ISBN 978-1-78148-613-9

ONE HUNDRED AND FIFTY
SHARDS OF LIGHT

INTRODUCTION

One of the pleasures of dining in a restaurant is spending time reviewing the menu. My wife is an expert. I can be ready to order within 30 seconds of receiving the menu. My wife will still be on page 1 of a 3 page menu because she enjoys the review. It's a bit like that with the Bible. There are so many stories there that deciding what to include in a book such as this is both a pleasure and time-consuming. However, the choice has been made. I hope you enjoy it.

The 150 articles that make up the book surfaced as a result of the challenge of writing them for the Parish Magazine produced on behalf of St Andrew's Church, Oxshott in the County of Surrey. The magazine only appears monthly, ten times a year. But, once I started writing the articles they poured out at a rate of about three a week over the space of a year, hence this book. Otherwise it would have taken over 13 years for all of the articles to have seen the light of day – and I'm not sure I am going to be around that long!

It was Winston Churchill, I believe, who once wrote "I am sorry this letter is so long. I did not have time to write a short one." Compressing stories inspired by the Holy

Spirit, to whom this book is dedicated, and the Bible into a maximum of 425 words per article is a challenge. In meeting that challenge I have taken liberties. That is why I have included a biblical reference at the top of those articles that allow for it, in the hope that readers will pursue the "official" version of what actually happened in that story. Read on!

SHADES OF
LIGHT – OLD TESTAMENT

Genesis 1

Son: "I'm reading the first chapter of Genesis, in the Bible. It tells how the earth and everything on it was created. What does modern science think about something written some 3,500 years ago?

Dad: "A very good question. I happen to have a book on that subject written by a Dr Hugh Ross. He's got a B.Sc in physics, an M.Sc and Ph.D in astronomy and was, for several years a post-doctoral fellow at the California Institute of Technology, researching quasars and galaxies. He's one astro-physicist amongst many and of course you get differing opinions. So I'll confine myself to quoting something he wrote that is universally agreed - the order in which things were made:

1. creation of the physical universe (space, time, matter, energy, galaxies, stars, planets, etc.);
2. transformation of the earth's atmosphere from opaque to translucent;
3. formation of a stable water cycle;

1

4. establishment of continent(s) and ocean(s);
5. production of plants on the continent(s);
6. transformation of the atmosphere from translucent to transparent (sun,moon and stars become visible for the first time);
7. production of small sea animals;
8. creation of sea mammals
9. creation of birds (possibly same time as 8);
10. making of land mammals (wild mammals and mammals capable of being domesticated, rodents)
11. creation of mankind.

Dr Ross added: "The record given in this table perfectly accords with the findings of modern science. The odds that Moses (who most theologians think probably wrote Genesis) could have guessed this correct order of events, even if he were given the events, are one chance in roughly 40 million." That's a lot worse than winning on the lottery! He goes on, "in addition, Moses scored three out of three in describing the initial conditions. Of course, most amazing of all is the accuracy of his depiction of each creative event. Moses must have been inspired by God to write as he did.""

Son: "How do we know that Moses was inspired by God? I realise the odds are extremely long but it is possible that chance played a part, isn't it?"

Dad: "Well, there are some clues. Moses tells us that God spoke to him out of the burning bush. He also met God when he was up Mount Sinai. He would meet regularly with God during the Israelites' journey through the desert. You would have to throw out the whole Bible if

you can't allow God a presence throughout its history."
You wouldn't want to do that, would you?"

YOU WANT ME TO DO WHAT?

Genesis 6

I am lost, now, in the mists of time but my life was just as important to me as yours is to you. In some ways we were better off. Our lives moved at a slower pace. We had time to really talk to each other and get to know each other pretty well. I knew all my neighbours. I bet you don't. We all worked with our hands. I was a carpenter. Each generation would succeed the other in the skills we developed. We didn't throw much away. It was amazing how adept we became at putting odds and ends to use. Can you say that of your modern society? If we were ill and couldn't work then everyone rallied round.

Sadly, it wasn't all sweetness and light. We might be happily working away living out our lives when over the hill would come a marauding band of villains. We didn't know they were coming. How could we? We didn't have telephones or cars. We couldn't escape. We just had to put up with whatever happened. Usually it was the ravaging of our flocks and grain which meant we had to start all over again. That's why we developed secret hiding places for grain and tools.

I have to admit that things in our society had started to break down quite badly. In fact, truth to tell, things were actually pretty bad. For a start, the cost of everything had become ridiculous. Always going up, never coming down. Traders were using dishonest scales. The quality of clothing had deteriorated. Coats that you used to wear for decades wore out in two or three years. We were becoming a society of cheats.

Far worse than that was the amount of sexual immorality going on. No-one seemed to mind who did what to whom. Wives and mothers were assaulted and then abandoned. Burglary and drunkenness were rife. You locked your doors and kept your heads down when young men and women went on drinking sprees and their behaviour! I could go on but I find it too distressing. I worried for my children and grandchildren. Would they succumb to the temptations that were prevalent?

As it happens, I wasn't the only one who found the whole thing distressing. God was upset as well. How did I know? Because he told me He was going to do something about it and I could help by building an ark. My initial response was one of surprise. "You want me to do what?"

ONE MISTAKE AFTER ANOTHER

Genesis 19

Abraham offered Lot the choice of where to settle and he chose to end up in the city of Sodom. It's true he got on well with the residents, most of the time, even as far as I know, becoming one of the city council members. At the same time he couldn't have been blind to the disgusting behaviour that was prevalent across the city – sexual immorality in all its forms. The worst behaviour of all was the way men lusted indiscriminately after other men.

This all came to a head when these two strangers came into town. There was something unusual about them, something menacing, although they were quite friendly to my sister and me when Lot, our Dad, invited them to stay the night. How menacing they were became clear shortly after they entered our house. The men of the city knew they were here and congregated outside our front door, demanding that the visitors be brought out so that they could have sex with them. How disgusting is that? But what do you think Dad did? Although we were both engaged to be married, he offered to send my sister and me out instead to satisfy their lusts, calling them his friends!

Fortunately the strangers pulled Dad into the house and stopped him making a disastrous mistake. They then blinded the men who were trying to break our door down. Scared? I could hardly move. Who were these strangers? It got worse when they told us that they had come to destroy Sodom and everyone in it. I could hardly sleep a wink.

The next morning the strangers got us up before sunrise and told us it was time to leave the city. We'd asked our prospective husbands to join us. They thought we were joking. We packed what we could and made our way to a nearby village. We were told not to look back but Mum disobeyed the instruction and got turned into a pillar of salt. So now it was just Dad and the two of us.

We eventually ended up living in a cave. Dad was the only man around so one night we got him drunk and then I slept with him. We did the same the next night. This time my sister slept with him. We both got pregnant. Alright, I know we shouldn't have and, looking back now, I can see that Abraham's descendants suffered from our mistake. Our descendants became the Moabites and Ammonites, deadly enemies of Israel.

THE TEST

Genesis 22

I was a bit of a spoilt brat. Well, my parents were at least one hundred years old when I was born. No, I don't know how it's possible but my dad tells me it's something to do with God. Apparently God is going to make a nation out of my Dad's offspring. That's me. So we don't want anything untoward to happen to me, do we?

So how do you explain what Dad got up to the other day? I can tell you I would never have taken part if he'd told me beforehand what was to happen. But he didn't, so I didn't suspect anything. It all came out later. Apparently God had decided to test Dad. So he told him to take me on a trip to the region of Moriah where he was to sacrifice me on one of the mountains there. That's right, me! The way Dad put it I thought I was going on a camping trip and we were going to do a bit of bonding. I was really excited.

So we got up early the next morning and set off with a donkey and two servants.

It was after we had been travelling for three days that I got the first inkling that something unusual was going on. Dad decided that we were approaching a place that was suitable for worship so he told the servants to stay with the donkey while we went on. I wanted to know what was going on but Dad wouldn't answer any of my questions. So we kept on trudging up the mountain.

Then he started glancing at me in a sorrowful sort of way, looking away whenever I saw him doing it. I was beginning to get worried. Finally I'd had enough. "Dad," I said, "We've got the wood and the fire but where's the sacrifice?" All Dad said was "God will provide." Then, when we got to the place of worship Dad built an altar. Then he suddenly turns on me, binds me up and throws me on the altar. I'm the sacrifice!

Needless to say I start screaming "Stop! Stop!" It's no good. Dad reaches for his knife and raises it to slay me. It's all over for me. Except an angel appears and tells Dad to stop. Dad had passed the test with flying colours.

I'm still reeling from the shock of it. Dad did explain everything to me on the way home but for several days afterwards I kept well clear of him.

I'M AFRAID THAT'S WHO I WAS

Genesis 27-31

Look, I didn't ask to be called Jacob, did I? You know what that name means? "He deceives". I don't think that's very nice. Do you? So now you want to know if I lived up to my name?

First of all there was the way I made Esau give me his birthright. He came in one day faint with hunger so I made him hand it over in exchange for some stew. Cheap at the price. Then, with the help of my mother, I deceived my father when he was virtually on his deathbed into thinking I was Esau so that he gave me the blessings intended for the elder son. I know. It wasn't very nice. You don't need to tell me.

Anyway, Esau let it be known that he was going to finish me off as soon as the period of mourning for our father was over. So my mother dispatched me off to her brother Laban in Haran, well out of the way. Needless to say, my behaviour didn't change when I got there but I have to admit that in Laban I met my match.

Once I got to Haran I fell in love with Laban's younger daughter, Rachel. She was a real looker, lovely in form and beautiful. I didn't much fancy Leah the elder sister because she had weak eyes. So I said I would work seven years in return for Rachel and I did. Then we had the wedding feast and so to bed. Guess what? The next morning there was Leah in my bed! What a trick! If it had been me that had arranged that I would have even impressed myself. Laban did give me Rachel as well but I then had to work another seven years for her. During that time Laban changed my wages no less than ten times! But I got my own back. I agreed with Laban that I would look after his flocks keeping only for myself any lambs that were speckled or spotted. I did that for six years.

I fixed it so that all the lambs the flock produced were speckled or spotted. So, Laban's flocks got smaller whilst mine got bigger. I became quite wealthy. After twenty years of work I decided to go home and left with all my possessions and family without saying a word to Laban. I had the last laugh there. So that's who I was. Then, on the way home things changed. You don't mind calling me Israel now?

AN AMAZING STORY (1)

Genesis 29-33

I don't suppose there's a book anywhere in the world that is quite as amazing as the Bible. My story appears in it. On its own my story would be amazing but, taken with the other stories in the Bible, mine is just one story among many.

I suppose I had better start with my Dad. This means I won't be able to get everything onto one sheet of paper – or even three! His name was Jacob and, in his youth he was a bit of a weasel. He really roughed up his brother Esau. Not in a physical sense, you understand. No, Esau was too physically well-endowed for that. But he was a bit slow on the uptake and that's where my Dad scored heavily. You see Dad was pretty smart. First he stole Esau's birthright from him. Then he stole his Dad's blessing for Esau. He did it by disguising himself as Esau, would you believe, and I don't think my Grandma, Rebekah, was entirely innocent in the affair either.

Well, the net result of all that was that Esau was hopping mad and clearly intended to have a sorting out with my Dad. So Grandma packs him off to her family in Haran, in northern Syria to stay with his Uncle Laban. I haven't got time to go into all the details of what he got up to there. I can, however, tell you that even though I wasn't born then it was the start of all my problems. First of all Jacob falls in love with one woman, Rachel, works seven years to earn her but ends up sleeping with her sister, Leah, on his wedding night. I mean, was he drunk or what? After that wedding week was over Jacob then marries Rachel, the girl he wanted to marry in the first place. Only now he's got to work another seven years to pay for her. Now we get into problems with babies. You've got to follow this closely because it gets complicated.

Leah produces four sons but Rachel can't produce any, so she gives Jacob her maidservant, Bilhah, to sleep with instead. Bilhah produces two sons – that's six so far. Now Leah gets jealous because she's not producing any more children so she gives her maidservant, Zilpah, to Jacob to sleep with instead of her. Zilpah produces two sons. So now we're up to eight sons. Still with me? We're not there yet. Believe it or not, Leah does a deal with Rachel the end result of which is that Jacob is obliged to sleep with Leah and, hey presto! another two sons appear. Ten and counting! After all that, we finally have a girl in the family, thanks to Leah. Anyway, back to Rachel and, yes, finally, she produces one son that's me, Joseph, and then another and that's Benjamin. He's the last. As you can imagine, we're a pretty dysfunctional family, what with two of Laban's daughters as wives, two of their maidservants as concubines, twelve sons between the four of them and only one daughter.

As we've now been with Laban for twenty years, Jacob thinks it might be safe to return home. He's still a bit of a weasel because he just makes off with his flocks and herds without telling Laban. He's also still a bit afraid of Esau so he puts together a huge bribe, in the shape of flocks and herds, in the hope of placating him even though, as it turns out, it isn't necessary. On the way home, something happens to Jacob. Now he's called Israel and he's a lot straighter all round but he won't tell us how that came about. Now it's time to get on to me.

AN AMAZING STORY (2)

I don't think I was very likeable in my teens. I used to sneak on my half-brothers. Unsurprisingly, this didn't go down well with them. Nor did the fact that I was Jacob's, sorry, Israel's favourite. (I'll call him Dad to avoid confusion). Nor did the fact that Dad made me a really super, richly ornamented robe that none of the others had. They really hated me for all of that and we didn't have a kind word to say between us. Things came to the boil when I had a couple of dreams all about them bowing down to me. As you can imagine, I wasn't slow in telling my dreams to them and Dad. Talk about gnashing of teeth! It just made me laugh.

Perhaps you can now understand what happened next. Dad sent me off to see if all was well with my half-brothers who were looking after the flocks. They saw me coming and, as there was no Dad around to keep an eye on them they dump me in a cistern, taking care to remove my robe first. Fortunately the cistern was dry although there were a few scorpions around that I had to keep an eye on. I assumed they wouldn't just leave me there and, sure enough, after a while they hauled me up again. Only, instead of having a laugh at my expense they flog me off to a passing Midianite trading caravan who take me to Egypt and sell me to one Potiphar, a high up in Pharaoh's court and captain of his guard. So, I am no longer a favoured member of a wealthy family; I am a rotten slave in a foreign country! How low can you get? Well, I am just about to find out.

I'd actually fallen on my feet. Potiphar lived in a rather upmarket mansion, with plenty of slaves to look after the needs of himself and his wife. She was quite a looker, by the way. Anyway, I had decided that the only way to get out of this mess was to work my way out by earning my freedom. So I kept my nose clean, stayed out of trouble and worked really hard. It was all going to plan and, you know what? I really felt that God was with me because I was successful at everything I was given to do. This even included becoming Potiphar's personal attendant. The zenith of my career came when Potiphar put me in charge of the entire house and the running of it. Here again, God was with me because everything got blessed. It was a very happy house.

There was one problem, however. That was Potiphar's wife. She started taking an interest in me and it wasn't a healthy one either. She would do silly little things, like making eyes at me across the room, brushing past me in the hall, so arranging things that we were alone in the same room together. I just ignored it to start with. Then it got more blatant. Eventually it was "Come to bed with me." And not just occasionally but every day. It started to get on my nerves. I explained to her as gently as I could that there was no way I was going to betray my master's confidence. It didn't stop her. In fact, things got so bad that I refused to have anything to do with her or be alone in the same room as her.

Then something dreadful happened. I went into the house not knowing that all the servants had gone out. She was there. No sooner did I enter than she seized hold of my cloak and started with the "Come to bed with me" again. I didn't stop but ran straight out of the house, leaving my cloak in her hands. This infuriated her and she turned against me. She told a pack of lies to the other servants about how I had tried to force myself on her, that she'd screamed and I'd fled. Then, when Potiphar returned home, she repeated the same pack of lies to him. It was no good my defending myself. Who was he going to believe, a slave or his wife? So I got packed off to prison. All my plans had come to naught over one stupid mistake. I would probably have ended it all there in misery and squalor but for one thing. God was with me.

AN AMAZING STORY (3)

I found favour with the prison warder. He put me in charge of all the prisoners and everything that went on in the prison. Because God was with me I was darned good at what I did. So, although I was in prison, life was at least reasonably tolerable. Then these two chumps turn up. One's a chief baker; the other's a chief cupbearer. They've managed to make Pharaoh angry – never a smart thing to do. Now they find themselves stuck in prison along with me.

One night they both have dreams. Now, you probably know that dreams were taken very seriously in our day. So it could be rather depressing if there was no-one around to interpret them. That's why these two were looking dejected. "Well, cheer up," I said. "Don't interpretations belong to God? Tell me your dreams." I was quite happy to deal with the cupbearer's dream. "In three days' time you'll get your old position back," I told him. That cheered him up no end. "But please, please use your new favourable position to get me out of this place. I know everyone says it, but I really haven't done anything to warrant my being stuck in here." He said he would but of course he totally forgot. As for the baker, he hadn't a hope. And sure enough, he lost his head three days later, just as I foretold.

So another two dreary years go by. I think God was teaching me patience or something because I was quite resigned to my lot when one morning I get a message from the Chief Warder that no less a person than Pharaoh wants to see me. I quickly shave, change my clothes and appear before Pharaoh. I can see Potiphar standing at the back but just ignore him. It seems that Pharaoh had also had a couple of dreams that no-one could interpret. At that point the wretched cupbearer remembered me and saw an opportunity to do himself a favour. So he told Pharaoh about my, or rather God's, ability to interpret dreams.

Sure enough, God gives me the interpretation. I tell Pharaoh that there are going to be seven years of plenty followed by seven years of famine. So he'd better get organised and store up the surplus for when the bad years come. The next thing you know God has put me in charge. Yes, he uses Pharaoh to order that I will be in charge of his palace and everyone, absolutely everyone, must submit to my orders. How's that for a quick change of scenery? God is not only amazing, he can arrange anything. As Pharaoh put it, "Only with respect to the throne will I be greater than you."

Let me tell you what that meant. First Pharaoh puts me in charge of the whole land of Egypt. Then he gives me his signet ring, dresses me in robes of fine linen and puts a gold chain round my neck. How the fallen become mighty! I then ride around in a chariot as Pharaoh's second-in-command with men shouting before me "Make Way!" Even better, Pharaoh gives me a wife from the priestly family of On – a real high born lady - and, can you believe, even better looking than Potiphar's wife. And, you know what? I was just thirty years old! Things just couldn't get any better, could they? Well, they did.

AN AMAZING STORY (4)

The seven years of plenty soon became seven years of famine and that famine spread right across the region, even into Canaan, where my family was living. They hear that there's grain to be had in Egypt so Dad, yes he's getting on a bit but he's still alive, sends the sons down to get some, keeping Benjamin at home. You could have knocked me down with a feather when I saw them trooping up to the grain stores. I recognised them immediately but they didn't recognise me. How could they? They probably thought I'd died from an overworked slavery. They certainly wouldn't be expecting me to turn up as Pharaoh's right hand man. Anyway, they all bowed down to me, just as the dream foretold. God was pressing on me to let bygones be bygones but I couldn't resist having a little fun with them. You know, for old time's sake? So I told them that one of them would have to stay in prison – nice touch, I thought – whilst the others went back to get Benjamin.

To cut a long story short, I did eventually disclose my true identity to them and we were reconciled. I also arranged for them all to come and live with me in Egypt. I was even was able to greet Dad before he died. What I told them when I looked back over it all was that God meant everything that happened to me for good. I saw his hand in everything. He is amazing and he gave me an amazing story to tell, didn't he?

SYMMETRY – SLAVERY

Genesis 47; Exodus 1

The Bible's full of symmetry, some of it quite unexpected. Take slavery, for example.

Back in 1898 B.C. Joseph was sold by his brothers, of all people, to a bunch of itinerant Midians, who were on their way to Egypt to sell their spices, balm and myrrh. When they arrived they sold Joseph as a slave to Potiphar, an Egyptian official. So Joseph knew all about slavery. Do you think his experience might have had an impact on how he dealt with matters in due course? The thing is, God rescued Joseph from prison and put him in charge of the whole of Egypt. He did this through giving Joseph the interpretation of Pharoah's dream about seven years of plenty followed by seven years of famine. And what a famine it was.

Fortunately, in Egypt, Joseph had stored up grain from the good years and so the Egyptians could cope with most of the famine. Towards the end of the seven years, however, the Egyptians had handed over to Joseph all the money that was to be found in Egypt and Canaan, in payment for the grain they were buying. But the famine went on. Now the Egyptians had no more money with which to buy grain. They came to Joseph and demanded food. As they had no money to buy the food Joseph took all their livestock - horses, sheep, goats, cattle and donkeys. That got them through the next year but still the famine persisted. What else could be used to buy grain now that all the Egyptians assets were owned by Pharaoh?

"We cannot hide from our lord the fact that since our money is gone and our livestock belongs to you, there is nothing left for our lord except our bodies and our land....Buy us and our land in exchange for food and we, with our land, will be in bondage to Pharaoh." That's what happened. The land became Pharaoh's and Joseph reduced the entire nation of Egypt to servitude.

Some four hundred years later we find roles have reversed. Now we have the Israelites, who started out as seventy strong when Joseph ruled on behalf of Pharaoh, in servitude to the Egyptians. The reason, this time, was not a famine but a feast, so to speak. The Israelites had prospered and flourished during those centuries and were now seen by the Egyptians as a threat to their well-being. We know a lot about one side of the coin but not much about the other, but it's there. Symmetry?

JOB – THE GREAT ENIGMA

Job

On the surface it's a simple story. Satan challenges God to let him test Job. He does this in a fearful manner, down to killing all his children and leaving Job with nothing but a distressing sickness, a depressed wife and three accusatory friends. In spite of the exhortations of his wife and friends, Job doesn't forsake God throughout his tribulations and is eventually restored to twice his former position of wealth and comfort.

If we look a little deeper we see some disturbing messages. The first is that none of us is immune to the wiles and damage that Satan can inflict. Satan's aim is now and always has been to separate man from God. "Worship me," said Satan to Jesus. What a triumph that would have been to separate Jesus from his Father. Happily, Jesus had his eyes on God and resisted Satan. "Curse God and die," said Job's wife to him. Happily Job kept his eyes on God. Do you think Satan is doing rather better in our day and age?

The second message is that things happen and not always for good. Job prayed daily for his children in case they might have sinned. We don't know if they prayed themselves but it is not unknown for godly men to have ungodly children. Think of Samuel. To all intents and purposes those prayers were brought to nothing when the servant reported to Job that a mighty wind had blown in from the desert and struck the house where Job's children were gathered. They all died. What must Job have thought when he heard his daily prayers had come, as he saw it, to naught? How often do we hear the argument "How could God, if there is a God, allow such a thing to happen?" How often do we find that our own prayers go unanswered, at least in the way that we would like? Are you praying for a job, any job? Forgive the unintended pun. Are you and your friends praying for healing from an illness? Are there dark days when you feel God isn't listening to you, doesn't care for you? As Job sat in the dust, picking at the sore scabs that covered him mightn't he have had doubts?

Have you heard of the prosperity gospel? It's often preached by TV evangelists. I get the impression they appear to maintain that, by putting your faith In God, and sending your prayer requests, with money, to them no harm will come your way. Would I be right in thinking they don't often preach about Job?

TEN MEN WHO DESTROYED A GENERATION

Numbers 13

This is the first chance we've had to review what happened down on earth, so think carefully before you answer. I'll set out the position and then you can have your turn.

You Israelites were slaves in Egypt. Moses was sent by God to lead you out of slavery into the promised land of Canaan. Through a series of perverse miraculous events, culminating in the deaths of the first born of his nation, Pharaoh agreed to let you go. After you'd left, Pharoah changed his mind. You'd only got to the Red Sea when his army appeared. It looked hopeless but God parted the Sea and you crossed it on dry land. When the Egyptian army followed it drowned.

Then there was the issue of food. You'd run out of it, so God provided quail in the evening and manna in the morning. Then, when you couldn't find any water in the desert, God provided it. When the Amalekites came to attack you God helped you to defeat them. It must have been clear that with God nothing is impossible.

But how fickle you Israelites were! When Moses disappeared up Mount Sinai you all thought he'd gone forever, and started worshipping a golden calf that Aaron had made. Was it because you thought that God was all kindness and soft? Had you forgotten that he had a hard edge to him, how he had punished the Egyptians to persuade them to let you go? Well, you paid for that error soon enough. So we have a situation where you are aware that God looks after you in astonishing ways but punishes you if you disobey.

That sets the scene for what follows. Moses brings you to the border of Canaan and then selects you heads of your tribes to explore the land that God has given you to occupy. You do that but when you return you bring back a report that says we can't go in because the people there are bigger and stronger than us. I'm leaving Joshua and Caleb out of this. You have forgotten that with God nothing is impossible.

You have treated him with contempt. So what happened? First of all, you ten get struck down and die of plague. Then the Israelites try to enter Canaan in their own strength. That fails. Then they spend forty years in the wilderness until that whole generation that wouldn't enter Canaan has died out. It seems to me that it was you who caused the death of that generation.

Now what's your take on that?

FEEL SORRY FOR MOSES?

What a story! This is how it starts. Moses is born to an Israelite mother in Egypt. This was at a time when the Egyptians, who had initially welcomed seventy Israelites among them, were now worried by the way they had flourished over the centuries and considered them a threat. So they came up with the brutal but practical idea of reducing their numbers by killing off all the new-born males. Moses' mother can't bear to lose her new-born baby boy so she hides him for three months. When she can hide him no longer she puts him in a papyrus basket, coated with tar and pitch, and launches him into the reed thickets of the River Nile.

I won't go into all the details of the matter but I can tell you that Pharaoh's daughter finds him and takes him under her wing, so to speak. It was she who gave Moses his name, meaning "I drew him out of the water." So Moses grows up in the household of Pharaoh, presumably benefitting from all the privileges offered by that lifestyle and reaches the age of forty.

However, Moses doesn't lose sight of the fact that he is really an Israelite. So when he sees an Egyptian fighting with one of his own he kills him. As a result Pharoah tries to have him killed, so he flees across the deserts of Sinai and Arabia until he reaches the safety and exile of Midian on the north-west of the Arabian peninsula.

Forty years pass. Moses is now eighty years old and, yes, he's a shepherd. It was while he was looking after his father-in-law's sheep that he sees an extraordinary sight – a bush burning without being consumed by the fire. It is here that Moses has his first encounter with God and receives his commission to lead the Israelites out of Egypt. After much argument with God Moses reluctantly accepts the challenge and returns to Egypt. There he becomes the spokesman for the Israelites, seeking to persuade Pharaoh to let them leave Egypt.

It takes the dreadful imposition of no less than ten plagues, culminating in the death of all the Egyptian first-born, before Pharoah realises that he is opposing the will of someone mightier than himself and lets the Israelites leave. Even then, Pharaoh is furious that they have gone and sends his army in pursuit – to no avail. Moses waves his staff and the waters of the Sea part to allow the Israelites a way through. Not so the Egyptian army. When they try to cross the Sea it closes back over them and the whole army perishes.

Now Moses finds himself in charge of something in the order of two million Israelites. He needs help. It comes from God who takes him up Mount Sinai and, over a period of forty days, gives him the commandments, rules and regulations needed to enable the Israelites, provided they adhere to them, to become a nation through whom all other nations will be blessed.

FEEL SORRY FOR MOSES? (2)

The adventures that the Israelites experience on their journey through the dreadful desert to reach the Promised Land are all set out in the Book of Exodus. They reveal how fickle and easily distracted the Israelites are. Time and again Moses has to intercede for them to prevent God from destroying them.

Can you imagine how disappointed Moses must have been when they finally arrived on the border of Canaan where they were to go in to destroy the inhabitants and take possession of the land? A scouting party reports back that the task is impossible so the Israelites refuse to enter the land. The net result of that refusal is that the Israelites will now spend the next forty years tramping around the desert until every member of the generation that refused to obey God and enter the land has died out. Moses will be one hundred and twenty years old before he can actually lead the Israelites to their destiny.

Is it any wonder that he finally gets fed up with the people he is leading? Yet again they are moaning. This time it's about the fact that there is no water for them to drink. God tells Moses to speak to a rock from which water will then pour, thereby bringing glory to God. Moses, however, chooses to use the occasion to berate the Israelites and make it look as though it is he who is making the rock produce water. Instead of speaking to the rock he strikes it, saying, "Listen you rebels, must we bring you water out of this rock?"

God's response is immediate. "Because you did not trust in me enough to honour me as holy in the sight of the Israelites, you will not bring this community into the land I give them."

Forty years growing up in Egypt, forty years as a refugee in Midian, forty years in the desert and all Moses is allowed is a glimpse of the Promised Land from the top of Mount Nebo, opposite the River Jordan and the city of Jericho. What's more, God tells Moses that the Israelites won't be able to obey the laws that will ensure their well-being and that they will suffer devastation. So he must have wondered what the last forty years were all about. Anyway, it is there on that mountain that Moses dies. Don't you feel sorry for him? I would but for one thing.

When Jesus takes his disciples - Peter, James and John – to the top of a high mountain and is transfigured, perhaps showing his disciples a glimpse of what awaits them in heaven, who was seen talking to him? Why, none other than Moses. Moses had suffered a temporal loss but had received a better reward - an eternal future with Jesus.

I don't feel sorry for Moses.

I COULDN'T BELIEVE MY EYES

Joshua 3

If you're sixteen years old you're a man. I was sixteen.

I was very proud that I had been chosen for this mission, which was to spy on the people who had arrived east of the Jordan River and were heading our way. I think it was because I had won the long distance race this year. I was pretty proud of that. Over six hundred of us had taken part. My tactics were to race off at the start and then hang on as best I could. However, I left everyone behind. But I'm digressing.

Haslem and I had reached a hillock overlooking the river, plonked ourselves down behind some reeds and crawled forward until we could see out. What we saw was quite extraordinary. First of all there was this enormous mass of people. I gave up counting when I got to 100,00 but I reckon there were at least six times that number of fighting men, let alone other hangers on – wives, children, cart drivers, etc. Thank goodness Jericho has got stout walls. But that wasn't what made the whole thing extraordinary. It was what happened next.

The ranks of the soldiers parted and through them appeared a group of what looked like priests, carrying a box. They walked down to the water's edge, stopped and appeared to be waiting. I'm not surprised. The river was in full spate and there's not much chance of them being able to cross it without boats. Except, to my total amazement the water in the river, which is flowing rapidly, starts dwindling until it stops altogether.

Then the priests move forward onto the river bed, which is totally dry, and stand in the middle of what used to be the river. At that point the mass of soldiers starts crossing over. On the way twelve of them stoop to pick up rocks from the river bed. When they get to our side they put them down in a way that forms a sort of pillar.

The whole lot of them are now crossing and they're getting nearer and nearer to Haslem and me. As the last of them come over, we decide to beat a retreat and report back on what we've seen. Just as we're about to move off the priests carrying the box-type thing come up out of the river and it starts flowing again!

I don't know who their god is but we haven't got a hope against this lot.

YES, I AM THAT WOMAN

Joshua 2 and 6

We knew they were coming – millions of them. Our scouts had told us. Frankly, we were petrified. They had crossed the Jordan without getting their feet wet. Now how can you do that without having a really powerful god with you? They were just behind the hill. We'd seen the dust they been kicking up for some time. Now we could hear them.

So I'm staring anxiously out when my door bursts open and these two spies crash in. "Hide us and you and your family are safe." That's what they said. So I did. I hid them under some flax stalks on the roof. The authorities knew they had come to my house but I told them the men had left. Excuse me whilst I attend to a client. About half an hour? Now, where was I? Oh didn't I tell you I was a prostitute? Sorry. Anyway, they shoot off again and the next thing you know, this vast number of people is right outside our walls.

Still, even with those numbers it was going to be difficult for them to get in and who's to say that our god wasn't more powerful than theirs? Then they start doing something really odd. The whole lot of them perambulate round the walls of the city. That's it. They don't try anything. They don't make any sort of noise at all, apart from some trumpets. It's creepy. It takes them hours to get round. Then they just go back to staring at us. This goes on for six days! You can imagine how edgy we all were, to say nothing of running short of food.

Then the seventh day arrives and what a change! First of all, they don't just go round once; they keep going round for, I don't know, about 6 or 7 times. Then some trumpets sound. They give a loud shout - and the city wall collapses, taking with it most of our defenders. Now we know their god is more powerful than ours! We're defenceless. They rush in and seize the city. There then follows the most terrible slaughter of everyone including animals. My family came crowding into my house. We sat there, with our hands over our ears, waiting for the inevitable. They're getting nearer and nearer and then, suddenly, the front door bursts open. Standing there are the two spies with bloody swords in their hands.

They come over to me. "You hid us, didn't you?". And I say "Yes, I am that woman."

IS THIS THE BIBLE'S SECOND BEST LOVE STORY?

Ruth

A family living in Bethlehem and owning a field there decides to escape famine by fleeing to Moab, a country to the east of the Dead Sea. This family comprises a husband, a wife called Naomi and two sons. The two sons marry Moabite women. Then the husband and the two sons die. Naomi decides to return to Bethlehem where she does at least have some friends. She tries to persuade the Moabite women to stay behind but one, called Ruth, refuses to leave and returns with her.

Once there, Ruth ekes out a subsistence by gathering gleanings from the cornfields. The field she chooses to work in belongs to a relative of Naomi called Boaz. He's a bachelor. However, he is clearly attracted to Ruth and shows her kindness. This is reported back by Ruth. Naomi advises her to go and see where Boaz rests his head overnight on the threshing floor and then to lie at his feet. When Boaz awakens and finds Ruth there he realises she is actually making a statement in response to all the kindness he has shown her.

So Boaz decides to redeem the field that was Naomi's and her sons' inheritance. Why such an odd decision? Because, in so doing in accordance with the law of the land, Boaz also acquires the widow of the dead son i.e. Ruth. Ruth becomes Boaz's wife and gives birth to a son. Naomi's friends pronounce a blessing over the new-born child. *"May he become famous throughout Israel! He will renew your life and sustain you in your old age."*

That's the story. I haven't told it very well. It's much better if you read it. It's the Book of Ruth in the Old Testament and it's only four chapters long. You can probably read it in 20 minutes. But the interesting question is "Why is it in the Bible at all? What's it got to do with the history of Israel and its relationship with the God who gave them the land? The answer comes right at the end of the Book: *"Boaz was the father of Obed. Obed was the father of Jesse, Jesse was the father of David."*

King David was the greatest king to rule Israel. But not only was Ruth his great grandmother, she also appears in the genealogy of Jesus. Interestingly, not only did Jesus' genealogy include a Moabitess, it also apparently included a prostitute. There's room for everyone in Jesus' family. Even you.

ARE YOU DESPERATE?

2 Kings 6 and 7

The Israelites were. They'd been besieged by the Arameans. The siege had lasted so long that a donkey's head sold for eighty shekels of silver. If you don't think that's desperate, try this: a woman approaches the king for redress because she had agreed with another woman that they were so famished they would kill and cook her son one day and the other woman's son the next but although they had eaten her son the other woman had welched on the deal. Don't you just love the Bible? Talk about warts and all!

So how does this terrible famine end? Well, four men with leprosy are hanging about the city gate. They can't enter because leprosy was considered to be highly infectious in those days. There's no point in them staying there. As they put it so succinctly *"If we go into the city we'll die. If we stay here we die. Let's go over to the Arameans. If they spare us we live; if they kill us we die."* So they go over to the Arameans. When they get to the Aramean camp they find no-one there – absolutely no-one. This is how the Bible explains that fact *"The Lord had caused the Arameans to hear the sound of chariots and horses and a great army…"* So they all fled back to Damascus.

Our four heroes promptly start ransacking one of the tents, then another but not before they have had a lot to eat and drink. They carry away gold, silver and clothes and hide them. Then they stop. *"We're not doing right. This is a day of good news and we are keeping it to ourselves.*" So they go back to the city gate and shout out to the guards that the enemy has gone. Having checked the position for themselves, the besieged rush out of the city and fall on the Aramean camp. Nobody is buying a donkey's head any more. Nobody is killing their child.

What about now? Do we have good news? I mean do we have news that is so good that when people realise they're desperate they too will rush to avail themselves of it? Yes we do! And this is the good news that Jesus, the Son of God, took all our sin onto himself and paid the cost of it in the most terrible torment, pain and suffering. Believe in Jesus and, whilst the enemy might not stop besieging you, you will live. But are you desperate enough to hear the good news?

ARE YOU REALLY WORSE THAN I WAS?

2 Samuel 11 and 12

I was the youngest of eight sons and got all the worst jobs - mainly looking after our sheep – cold nights, fighting off wolves, bears and lions. One day, this old man comes to our village. The elders are scared stiff. He tells my dad to produce his sons. To the utter astonishment of myself and my family, he anoints me with oil and I get filled with the Spirit of the Lord.

The next thing? I am invited to King Saul's court to play my harp. My family still want me to look after the sheep, so I go back and forth. Then the wretched Philistines kick up a fuss. They've got this huge fellow, Goliath, who challenges us to one-to-one combat. No-one wants to fight him. Well, I've always been a bit impetuous. Anyway, I'm talking to my brothers when Goliath comes out and makes his challenge. Before you know it, I am responding. Well, we can't have him making a mockery of our God, the living God. So I pick up my sling run up to him and put a stone straight through his forehead. Down he goes and I cut off his head. Easy!

I then get into all sorts of trouble. King Saul knows that I am going to be the next King of Israel and keeps trying to kill me. It doesn't work. He dies and I claim the throne.

Now, I've always had an eye for a pretty girl. I married seven of them for goodness' sake. So, I'm up on the roof walking around and there's this stunning girl taking a bath on the next roof along – I mean right in front of my eyes. Well, I told you I was impetuous. I made inquiries and called for her. She was already married but, you know what? That didn't stop me – or her. We spent the night together. Soon after she tells me she's pregnant. So, after various unsuccessful attempts to get her husband to sleep with her, I arrange to have him killed in battle. Then I marry her and enjoy her company to my heart's content. I'm not very nice, am I?

It didn't work. Nathan the prophet knew it all. He said we would lose the child, which we did, and various other punishments would come my family's way, which they did. But I repented, paid my heavy dues and God forgave me. And God can do the same for you. Are you really worse than I was?

UPS AND DOWNS

Psalm 25

David had his problems. He was an adulterer and a murderer, amongst other things. The Bible doesn't, however, provide us with a complete record of David's life. We don't know what he liked for breakfast. Nor do we know about all the arguments he had with his family. There must have been some.

What we do know is that when David stopped and took stock of what was happening he turned to God in prayer. How else would he have been able to write the many psalms we are fortunate enough to be able to turn to ourselves when we are in need?

The one that springs to mind is Psalm 25. Could you have written this? Can you imagine the state David was in when he penned this psalm? It must have been one of those occasions when all the things he had done wrong rose up to flood his mind. Does that happen to you? Do you find yourself recalling things you wish you hadn't done, even though you know that Jesus died to wipe out those very sins? No wonder Paul, writing elsewhere in the Bible instructs us to renew our minds

"To you, O Lord, I lift up my soul; in you I trust O my
  God. Do not let me be put to shame nor let my
  enemies triumph over me...
Show me your ways, O Lord, teach me your paths; guide
  me in your truth and teach me for you are God my
  Saviour , and my hope is in you all day long...

33

Remember not the sins of my youth and my rebellious
ways; according to your love remember me, for you
are good, O Lord...
For the sake of your name, O Lord, forgive my iniquity,
though it is great...
Turn to me and be gracious to me, for I am lonely and
afflicted. The troubles of my heart have multiplied;
free me from my anguish...
Look upon my affliction and distress and take away all
my sins...
Guard my life and rescue me; let me not be put to
shame, for I take refuge in you... May integrity
and uprighteousness protect me, because my hope is
in you..."

David didn't waste any time. He prayed that prayer.
But he also wrote Psalm 26. It starts *"Vindicate me,*
O Lord, for I have led a blameless life..." He couldn't
have written those words unless he was confident his
prayer in Psalm 25 had been answered. Are you that
confident?

OBED –WHO?

2 Samuel 6

You don't know me. I'm Obed-Edom and I'm in the Old
Testament of the Bible. I wouldn't have got a mention
there if it wasn't for one terrible incident.

I was working in my vineyard when I heard this amazing
cacophony – harps, lyres, cymbals and trumpets – mixed
up with men singing and cheering, and the lowing of

oxen. I looked up the road to see what was happening. Right there, before my eyes, were King David and a mighty throng moving the ark of God to Jerusalem. Just as they were passing my plot the cart tilts over and one of the group puts his hand on the ark to steady it. The next thing you know, he's lying in the roadway, dead. God had struck him down for touching a holy thing.

Consternation all round. King David says he's scared to take the ark into Jerusalem, so they decide they're going to leave it on my plot! I hurriedly call together my family – me, my wife and daughter – and tell them they mustn't under any circumstances go near the ark, literally on pain of death. So there it sits for three months – and things start happening.

The Bible simply says the Lord blessed my household and everything I had. Have you any idea what that meant? If you think it's all about money, think again. How does God bless us? The answer is to look to Jesus. How did he bless people? He healed them. He performed miracles. He gave them superb catches of fish. He brought peace and comfort. He shared his wisdom with them. So, first of all I had the best crop of grapes I've ever had. Then both my pregnant oxen gave birth to healthy heifers. Then my wife's arthritis cleared up. Then my bad back got sorted out. Then my daughter's eyesight improved. Then I was invited to join the local leadership. There was no end to it. Things just got better and better.

King David gets to hear about this. I guess he must have thought if God can bless Obed-Edom just by having the ark on his plot then perhaps he can bless him, David, if he moves the ark to Jerusalem after all. So he moves the ark off my land. Do you think my blessings stopped at that point? Well, they didn't. You need to read 1 Chronicles, Chapter 26, verses 4-8. Not only did my darling wife produce 8 sons, described as capable men, but I had 62 descendants in total. Now how blessed is that?

WE CAN'T DO IT ALL OURSELVES

1 Kings 11

There are many people who believe that they can work life out for themselves, lead a happy and contented life and, subject to the minor inconvenience of death, go gaily and blindly into oblivion. Unfortunately, things over which we have no direct control intrude into this idyllic gallery of life and then things go wrong – higher taxes, lower pension payouts, noisy neighbours, drunk drivers, Asian flu, etc. It seems that, no matter at what level you review the situation there's always something lacking.

Take King Solomon of Israel. God gave him wisdom and Solomon became greater in riches and wisdom than all the other kings of the earth. All Solomon had to do was obey God's commands, the most important of which was to *"have no other gods before me"*. So what could possibly have gone wrong? It was this. Solomon clearly thought that his wisdom could be used to his advantage In the pursuit of his happy and contented life. *"King Solomon loved* (married) *many foreign women...they were from nations about which the Lord had told the Israelites, "You must not intermarry with them because they will turn your hearts after their gods."* And the result? *"...his wives turned his heart after other gods. He followed Ashtoreth, the goddess of the Sidonians and Molech, the detestable god of the Ammonites."*

When you think only of yourself and your personal aims in life things go wrong. It's finding out the hard way that we can't do it all ourselves. It may be that the happy and contented life you envisaged ends in divorce, financial hardship, separation from loved ones or depression. Goodness knows there's enough of that around at the moment. Or it may be that you do indeed lead your happy and contented life but then discover there is no such thing as oblivion, no matter how much you then wish there was.

So what went wrong for Solomon? God said *Since you have not kept my ... decrees...I will most certainly tear the kingdom away from you."* The result of the failings of the wisest man in the world was to leave Israel as a divided nation with one tribe, Judah, ruled by Solomon's family and the ten other tribes ruled by others. We all know the saying "A nation divided against itself cannot stand." Israel couldn't. Israel's history from then on was a story of civil war and diminution of power, concluding in the oblivion of exile.

You leave God out of the equation at your peril.

FROM JUDGES TO KINGS TO... DISASTER

2 Kings 10

Once the generation that took over the Promised Land had died, its place was taken by those who *"knew neither the Lord nor what he had done for them."* They forsook him and worshipped the various gods of the people around them. So what was the consequence? *"In his anger...the Lord handed them over to raiders who plundered them. He sold them to their enemies... whom they were no longer able to resist...They were in great distress."*

God however, in his great mercy, raised up judges who saved them out of the hands of these raiders. As long as a judge lived God protected the Israelites. Once that judge died and the people reverted to worshipping other gods, God left them to their misery, in-fighting amongst themselves and defeat at the hands of their enemies. These phases of judge and peace no judge and misery lasted about 350 years.

The last and probably the greatest of the judges was Samuel. He did appoint his two sons to be judges after him but they were corrupt, accepting bribes and perverting justice. As a result, they were rejected by the elders of Israel. These elders came to Samuel and asked him to appoint a king *"such as all the other nations have."* Samuel did the sensible thing and handed it over to God who told him: *"It is not you they have rejected, but they have rejected me as their king...Now listen to them, but warn them solemnly what the king who will reign over them will do."* This Samuel did, telling them of the burdens that a king would impose. They refused to listen to him and demanded a king.

That king was Saul. His tussles with David, who succeeded him are graphically described in the First Book of Kings in the Bible. David was Israel's greatest military figure of the Old Testament. Under his leadership Israel became an empire, stretching from the Mediterranean Sea to the Arabian desert and from the Red Sea to the Euphrates River. He was succeeded by Solomon. Sadly, it was Solomon who aroused God's anger by marrying an inordinate number of wives and maintaining a large number of concubines, all of whom brought with them their foreign gods and turned Solomon's heart away from God. As a result, Israel became divided into two states: Israel, the northern kingdom and Judah, the southern kingdom. To paraphrase Jesus: *"A kingdom divided will be ruined."* So it was to prove.

ARE YOU SICK AND TIRED OF PROPHETS?

2 Kings 22

Do you read the Old Testament part of the Bible? If you do you will see that it's made up of 39 books. Of those, 16 cover the writings and sayings of the prophets. It's not pretty reading. Almost from the time that Israel entered the Promised Land things started going downhill. The prophets saw it as their duty to relay to Israel God's warnings about this in the hope that things would improve.

There were kings who tried to halt and occasionally managed to turn back Israel's descent into destruction but their efforts didn't endure. The people's hearts were turned away from God. This, of course, meant that prophets who railed against their behaviour weren't very popular. Quite the reverse. Rulers became sick and tired of them. There was plenty of "shooting the messenger". Prophets were imprisoned, stoned, starved, cast into exile and generally mistreated. Yet they continued to speak out.

The very last prophet recorded in Chronicles - the history of Israel and Judah which forms part of the Old Testament - was a woman. This is how she comes to our attention. King Josiah had ascended to the throne of Judah in 639BC. In the 18th year of his reign the temple, which had fallen into disrepair, was restored. During this restoration a book was found, containing the law given to Moses by God around 1440BC. It was read to King Josiah who, when he heard what God's requirements were and being aware of the extent to which Israel had neglected them, tore his robes as a sign of his distress.

The King then sent Hilkiah, the chief priest, to see Huldah, a prophetess, who lived in Jerusalem and who was presumably well-known to the King. She didn't say much but what she did say was terrifying:

"This is what the Lord, the God of Israel, says: Tell the man who sent you to me... I am going to bring disaster on this place and its people – all the curses written in the book that has been read in the presence of the King.

Because they have forsaken me and burned incense to other gods and provoked me to anger by all their hands have made, my anger will be poured out on this place and will not be quenched."

Twenty-two years and six months later, the Babylonians invaded Judah and sacked Jerusalem, taking all but the meanest and poorest into exile.

We may be sick and tired of prophets but we ignore them at our peril.

YOU CAN'T BE A PROPHET IF YOU DON'T PROPHESY

1 Kings
2 Kings 23

Now, let me tell you about a real prophecy. Jeroboam had been appointed king over ten tribes of Israel, leaving only the tribe of Judah with King Rehoboam. To prevent the ten tribes, now called Israel, from returning to join with Judah in worshipping in Jerusalem, Jeroboam built two shrines to golden calves, one in Dan and the other at Bethel and required the people of the new state of Israel to worship there.

So, whilst Jeroboam is offering sacrifices on the altar he had built at Bethel, a prophet comes from Judah and "cries out against the altar by the word of the Lord *"O altar, altar! This is what the Lord says: "A son named Josiah will be born to the house of David. On you he will sacrifice the priests of the high places who now make offerings here, and human bones will be burned on you." This is the sign the Lord has declared: the altar will be split apart and the ashes on it will be poured out."* That's prophecy, isn't it? It's clear and it's measurable. And, sure enough, right at that moment the altar was split apart and its ashes poured out. That's pretty instantaneous prophecy, but who's Josiah and what's all this about bones being burned on the altar?

Jeroboam reigned over Israel from 930-909B.C. Some 300 years later Josiah, a descendant of King David became king of Judah reigning from 640-609B.C God's timings are not always the same as ours. This is how the Old Testament tells us this prophecy came to be fulfilled:

"Josiah was eight years old when he became king....he did what was right in the eyes of the Lord and walked in the ways of his father David..." He then set about destroying all the idols in the land and finally arrives at Bethel. *"Even the altar at Bethel, the high place made by Jeroboam son of Nebat, who had caused Israel to sin – even that altar and high place he demolished. He burned the high place and ground it to powder...Then Josiah looked around, and when he saw the tombs that were there on the hillside, he had the bones removed from them and burned on the altar to defile it, in accordance with the word of the Lord proclaimed by the man of God who foretold these things..."* – 300 years earlier.

Now that's some prophecy. Can anyone match that? Well, Jesus can....

THERE IS A GREATER POWER

2 Kings 19

So Hezekiah came to the throne of Judah when he was twenty-five, in 715B.C. He did what was right in the eyes of the Lord. He didn't hang about. In the first month of his first year as king he began the process of ridding the temple of anything unclean i.e. that related to the worship of other gods. He brought the people of Judah back into a proper relationship with God. He decided to hold a celebration of the Passover and invited everyone across the whole of Israel and Judah to attend. He really followed God and enjoyed the benefits of doing so. As the Bible tells us *"he sought his God and worked wholeheartedly. And so he prospered."*

Now, you would think that a God who enjoyed such devotion would protect Hezekiah and Judah from harm. In the same way you might think that those who follow Jesus would be kept free from the bad things that happen in our world today – disease, floods, sickness, financial harm and many more. After all, during other reigns in Israel and Judah we learn that the fear of Israel fell on the countries around them and they were left to live in peace and prosperity.

Unfortunately, that's not the way things always work. In Hezekiah's case, five hundred miles away a huge storm is brewing and it's heading for Jerusalem, conquering everything in its path. Its leader is Sennacherib, ruler of Assyria and he's coming with a huge army. He marches on Jerusalem. Hezekiah does everything he practically can to thwart Sennacherib - building additional defensive walls, stopping up all the springs and streams and so on. Of itself, that wouldn't have been enough to counter the storm. But what does the Bible say? In addition to working wholeheartedly Hezekiah sought his God.

This is how Hezekiah addressed his people at this time of acute danger, *"Be strong and courageous. Do not be afraid or discouraged because of the King of Assyria and the vast army with him, for there is a greater power with us than with him. With him is only the arm of flesh, but with us is the Lord our God to help us and fight our battles."*

So what happened? Hezekiah and the Prophet Isaiah cried out in prayer... *"and the Lord sent an angel who annihilated all the fighting men..their leaders and officers,"* Sennacherib returned to Assyria in disgrace and was assassinated. There is a greater power. Don't leave him out of your deliberations.

LET ME TELL YOU ABOUT.......MANASSEH

2 Kings 21

If you want to know at what point a loving God has had enough, take a look at Manasseh, King of Judah 697-642BC.

Manasseh reigned for 55 years. So he had plenty of time to stamp his awful mark on the kingdom. This is how he did it and so upset God that He determined to put an end to Judah. First of all he followed the detestable practices of the nations that God had driven out in order to create Israel. In other words, Judah was now behaving just like or even worse than those nations. So things were now no better than they had been all those years ago when God determined to destroy those nations. Then he erected altars to Baal and made an Asherah pole. That's a pole set up to worship the goddess Asherah. He bowed down to all the starry hosts and worshipped them. He even built altars to them in both courts of the temple of which God had said *"In Jerusalem I will put my name."* There's more but you need to read 2 Kings, chapter 21 to get the full flavour.

God was being ignored and discarded. Can you see why He was angry? Unfortunately, it gets worse. Manasseh sacrificed his own son in the fire by way of worship. What a terrible thing to do. Do you know why Christians consider abortion an abomination? Not only is the killing of a defenceless unborn child a disgusting and disgraceful thing to do, it also flouts God's command "Thou shalt not murder". Do you think God is angry with the fact that nearly 200,000 abortions took place in the UK in 2011? This is the God of whom it is said *"I knit you together in your mother's womb."* Manasseh also "shed so much innocent blood he filled Jerusalem from end to end."

So, let's see what an angry God decided to do. *"I will wipe out Jerusalem as one wipes out a dish...I will forsake the remnant of my inheritance and hand them over to their enemies. They will be looted and plundered by all their foes".* Although Manasseh finally repented of all his evil acts and sought to repair the damage, it was too little, too late. In 586BC the Babylonians came, sacked Jerusalem and carted off to exile what remnant there was, which was not saying much as the power, wealth and influence of Israel had virtually evaporated. God will not be mocked.

FROM TWO MILLION TO FOUR THOUSAND SIX HUNDRED

When the Israelites left Egypt in 1446BC they were about two million strong. Well, they might not have been strong militarily then but, by the time they entered the Promised Land they were battle-hardened. Every nation in the area was in awe, if not terror of them. They had everything going for them – a land of milk and honey, one victory after another and, most importantly, a God who cared for and protected them.

By the time Nebuchadnezzar and his hordes invaded and destroyed Jerusalem in 586BC, some 840 years later, there were only a pitiful four thousand six hundred left to take into exile. You need to read Lamentations to get a sense of the desolation: *"How deserted lies the city, once so full of people! How like a widow is she, who was once great amongst the nations! She who was queen among the provinces has now become a slave."* Where did it all go wrong?

When the Israelites first entered Israel they were commanded to split, with six tribes climbing to the top of Mount Gerizim to pronounce blessings and six to the top of Mount Ebal to pronounce curses. And what blessings and curses they were! *"If you fully obey the Lord your God and carefully follow all his commands... the Lord your God will set you high above all the nations on earth..."* How high? High above the empires of Greece, Rome and Britain, high above the might of America, China, India, Asia. With God nothing is impossible. But what about the curses? *"If you do not obey the Lord your God and do not carefully follow all his commands and decrees...The Lord will send on you curses, confusion and rebuke in everything you put your hand to, until you are destroyed and come to sudden ruin because of the evil you have done in forsaking him."*

That was a pretty clear choice. And the Israelites chose. First of all, they chose to disobey God's command to drive out the nations that were already occupying the land of Canaan. Instead, when they became strong enough, the Israelites made those nations forced labourers. This did not go unremarked: *"You have disobeyed me...now therefore I tell you I will not drive them out...they will be thorns in your sides and their gods will be a snare to you."* Oh dear. It all went wrong so quickly and, with the benefit of hindsight and the Bible, we can begin to see how and why.

WHO'D BE A PROPHET?

Jeremiah

The Prophets were raised by God, during the dark days of Israel, from about the 9th to the 4th centuries B.C. Their duty was to deal with moral and religious life.

Jeremiah was a prophet. He lived around 640-586BC. He may have been a descendant of Abiathar, a priest during the reign of King Solomon. At the age of 21 he was commissioned by God: *"Before I formed you in the womb I knew you, before you were born I set you apart. I appointed you as a prophet to the nations."* Perhaps rightly, Jeremiah was reluctant to take on the role: *"I do not know how to speak; I am only a child."* God assured him that he would be defended.

And so Jeremiah prophesied during the reigns of five kings of Judah. What was his message? First of all, he lashed out against the sins of his countrymen, rebuking them severely for their idolatry – worship of gods other than the true God, leading them even to sacrifice their children to foreign gods. God's judgment on Judah was also a constant theme, although Jeremiah did say that repentance would postpone the inevitable. He warned that Judah would be destroyed and advised submission to Babylon so as to enable the Israelites to carry on life as normal under them. God also commanded Jeremiah not to marry and raise children because of the impending divine judgment that would sweep away the next generation. He also prophesied that Israel's exile under the Babylonians would last 70 years, which is exactly what it did.

None of the above was popular and led to accusations that he was a traitor, worthy of death. On one occasion his enemies beat him and put him in prison. Jeremiah's story is typical of Israel's prophets. No wonder he was reluctant to take on the role.

It is a sobering thought that, if a prophet was to appear today, he would probably be arrested under anti-religious, anti-discrimination or hate crime laws. He would have no time for any religion other than the true faith in Christ Jesus. He would rage against the misdemeanours of bankers and politicians. He would have pungent views on abortion, homosexuality and other sexual variations. He would speak out against those who lived in palaces whilst the poor were mistreated. He would criticise the way the state looks after its old and young. He would end up in prison but he wouldn't stop speaking out just because of his arrest. Who'd be a prophet?

A SHORT "HISTORY" OF OLD TESTAMENT ISRAEL

Alright! Get fell in. Shortest on the left, tallest on the right. Come on. Get a move on! What a dozy lot you are! Now, let's check that you're all here and no-one's getting extra time in bed. Sound off. In no particular order: Solomon, Rehoboam, Jeroboam, Abijah, Asa, Nadab, Baasha, Zimri, Omri, Ahab, Ahaziah, Joram, Jehoram, Ahaziah, Jehu, Athaliah, Jehoahaz, Jehoash, Jeroboam II, Zechariah, Menahem, Pekahiah, Pekah, Ahaz, Hoshea, Manasseh, Amon, Jehoahaz, Asa, Jehoshaphat, Joash, Amaziah, Azariah, Shallum, Jotham, Hezekiah, Josiah, Jehoakim, Jehoachin, Zedekiah. Good. Now pay attention.

Today we're going to examine that interesting chapter in the history of Israel of how a country of great wealth, power and strength managed to ruin and destroy itself under your management. No, I didn't think you would like that but you've got no choice. It's either complete the course and move on or go back to the sorry lives you were leading before you arrived here. Your choice. Left to me, I know what I'd do with you miserable bunch. Happily for you I'm not in charge.

The title of this part of the course is called "Kings of Israel and Judah – and what went wrong". Right, let's start with you, Solomon. Step forward! Now let's see if I've got this right. When you came to the throne you prayed for wisdom and God answered your prayer. According to the Bible

> *"God gave (you) wisdom and very great insight, and a breadth of understanding as measureless as the sand on the seashore. (Your) wisdom was greater than all the wisdom of all the men of the East and greater than all the wisdom of Egypt. You were wiser than any other man ... and your fame spread to all the surrounding nations."*

So, you were a wise man. That's good to know but my next question is, if that was the case, why did you do some of the things you did? No. I don't need you to answer and I don't want to hear from any of the rest of you either. You'll all keep quiet. I will do the talking. In case you don't know, that was what we call a rhetorical question.

First of all you wrote Ecclesiastices. As I understand it, these are the writings based on your many years of wisdom. So, how do they start? *"Meaningless!*

Meaningless! Everything is meaningless! And how did you respond to that in Ecclesiastices? *"So, I hated life, because the work that is done under the sun was grievous to me."* I'm sorry? Everything is meaningless? Work was grievous to you? You hated life? What about the poor man down the road who had to beg for a living? What about the slaves and people you conscripted who actually did most of that work that was grievous? It seems to me that you'd lost sight of the God who loved you so much that he gave you wisdom and wealth to excess.

A SHORT "HISTORY" OF OLD TESTAMENT ISRAEL (2)

So, when I look at Chapter 2 of Ecclesiastices I come across the great "I". I undertook great projects. *I built houses. I planted gardens and made reservoirs. I bought slaves. I owned more herds and flocks than anyone before me. I amassed silver and gold for myself. I acquired a harem"*– we'll come back to that in a moment – *I became greater by far than anyone in Jerusalem before me. I denied myself nothing."* It's the great "I" isn't it? Where in any of that did you give God credit? Nowhere. You're lucky you didn't end up like Nebuchadnezzar. When he took all glory for building Babylon on himself God made him mad. Anyway, would it be true to say that, if you leave God out of the equation, life doesn't make sense? Is that why, at the end of your writings you add on this conclusion: *"Fear God and keep his commandments, for this is the whole duty of man"*?

So, my next question is "Why didn't you?" You knew that if you married women outside the tribes of Israel they would bring with them the foreign gods they worshipped. You knew that if they did bring their gods with them you would end up worshipping them instead of the one true God. So why did you marry no less than seven hundred of them and then go on to create a harem of 300 concubines? What was the point? In Ecclesiastices you write: *"I denied myself nothing my eyes desired; I refused my heart no pleasure."* Was that it? Every time you saw a pretty girl you couldn't keep your eyes or hands off her? So, what was the result? Your wives turned your heart away from God.

> *"The Lord became angry with Solomon because his heart had turned away from the Lord, the God of Israel, who had appeared to him twice. Although he had forbidden Solomon to follow other gods, Solomon did not keep the Lord's command."*

Well done, Solomon! Because of you God tore the kingdom away from you and gave it to one of your subordinates, leaving only one tribe, Judah, for your son to rule. You know what Jesus said? *"Every kingdom divided against itself will be ruined..."* You in your great wisdom knew all that but you still went ahead and disobeyed God. What a mess. Solomon, get back in the rank! Step forward Rehoboam and Jeroboam.

A SHORT "HISTORY" OF OLD TESTAMENT ISRAEL (3)

Now, let's see, Rehoboam. You know as well as I do that God is long-suffering and prepared to forgive. You know as well as I do the story of Sodom and Gomorrah, both vile places and worthy of the destruction that God intended for them. You know he was prepared to spare both places if only ten righteous people could be found there. You had the chance to put right the things that Solomon had messed up. You had the chance to get rid of the foreign gods and be reconciled with Jeroboam. In fact, Jeroboam gave you that chance because he came to you and offered to serve you, along with the ten tribes he represented, if you would only lighten the heavy yoke that Solomon had put upon them. Had you offered matters up to God you might have received the right advice. You didn't do that. You decided to make their yoke even heavier. Jeroboam wasn't going to put up with that, was he? So he left, taking the ten tribes with him. I can't say I blame him for that. But I do blame him for what happened next.

So now we have this wonderful temple built by Solomon where God is to be found amongst his chosen people. But you, Jeroboam, aren't happy with that situation, are you? You think that if your tribes carry on going to Jerusalem to worship at the temple they might eventually be reconciled to Judah and Israel would again be one nation. Well, you couldn't have that, could you? Where would that leave you and your cronies? Facing the death sentence, in all likelihood. So, what do you do? You have two golden calves made, put them up in Bethel and Dan and order the ten tribes to worship them rather than go to Jerusalem. How stupid is that? Didn't you learn anything from history? Aaron made a golden calf and it brought death and destruction. You make two. What do you think's going to happen? I'll tell you – death and destruction! Get back in the rank the pair of you!

A SHORT "HISTORY" OF OLD TESTAMENT ISRAEL (4)

All right, we're going to cut this short because, when I cover this bit of the course, I get angry and depressed and you don't want me angry and depressed. Step forward when I call your name out. Asa, Jehoshaphat, Joash, Amaziah, Azariah, Shallum, Jotham, Hezekiah, Josiah. You lot fall out and go and get some lunch. What happens next had nothing to do with you. Those of you who are left – a depressingly large number – listen carefully whilst I explain what went wrong. Actually, you are going to listen to a reading I recorded a few courses back. I made this recording because I get so churned up when I give the explanation live. It's from the Bible, so listen up.

"Israel exiled because of sin
(The exile of Israel) *took place because the Israelites had sinned against the Lord their God, who had brought them out of Egypt from under the power of Pharaoh king of Egypt. They worshipped other gods and followed the practices of the nations the Lord had driven out before them, as well as the practices that the kings of Israel had introduced.*

The Israelites secretly did things against the Lord their God that were not right. ...they built themselves high places...they set up sacred stones and Asherah poles... they did wicked things that provoked the Lord to anger. They worshipped idols, though the Lord had said "You shall not do this." They rejected the decrees and covenants the Lord had made with their fathers. They followed worthless idols and themselves became worthless. They forsook all the commands of ...their God and made...two idols cast in the shape of calves and an Asherah pole. They bowed down to all the starry hosts, and they worshipped Baal. They sacrificed their sons and daughters in the fire. They practised divination and sorcery and sold themselves to do evil in the eyes of the Lord, provoking him to anger.

So the Lord was very angry with Israel and removed them from his presence. Even Judah did not keep God's commands. They followed the practices that Israel had introduced. Therefore the Lord rejected all the people of Israel; he afflicted them and gave them into the hands of plunderers until he thrust them from his presence.....So the people of Israel were taken from their homeland into exile in Assyria, and they are still there."

I think that's clear enough, don't you? And all of that happened on your watches. You are a disgrace. Frankly I don't have the words to describe how I feel. Left to me you'd never get through this course. However, I have to hand you on to your next instructor. The reason I am doing so and the reason why I am saving your bacon is because of who you learn about on that part of the course. His name's Jesus and, let me tell you, you owe him everything. Now get out of here.

JOSEPH ISN'T THE ONLY ONE

Daniel

Joseph does make me laugh. I sometimes think that just because he's had a musical written about him and his technicolour coat he thinks his story is the most amazing in the Old Testament of the Bible. I can challenge that but I will say one thing. Have you noticed how often we Israelites turn up in the most unexpected and exalted places? Of course there was Joseph, the right hand man of Pharoah. But there was also Esther, queen to the King of Persia, ruler of over 127 provinces and Mordecai, his chief administrator. And then there was me, Daniel.

It was in about 605B.C. that Nebuchadnezzar, King of Babylon, came to Jerusalem and besieged it. Following that triumphant siege, he deported a lot of us, including me. Like Joseph, I was from a wealthy and influential family. We were nobles. However, we ended up in a rather depressing exile where I would probably have eked out a miserable existence as a farmer had it not been for an astonishing idea of King Nebuchadnezzar. He instructed his chief court official to bring in some of us Israelite men from the royal family and nobles. We had to be physically perfect, handsome, intelligent and quick on the uptake and knowledgeable about royal service. I was one of those chosen.

Over a period of three years we learned the language and read the literature of the Babylonians, familiarising ourselves with the ways of the palace. After the three years were up I entered the King's service. So far, my story's not dissimilar to Joseph rising to work for Pharaoh. In fact, Joseph and I were marching step for step because God not only gave me knowledge and understanding of all kinds of literature and learning, he also gave me understanding of visions and dreams, just like Joseph. Sure enough, the King had dreams.

These troubled him so he brought in his magicians, enchanters, sorcerers and astrologers. This, however, is where Joseph and I part company. Whereas Pharaoh told Joseph what his dreams were about, Nebuchadnezzar decided not to tell any of us what his dreams were. In fact, he ordered all the wise men of Babylon to be executed if no-one could tell him his dreams and interpret them for him. Well, that included me and my three close companions. So we did the sensible thing and turned to God for help. The night before we were due to be executed, God was kind enough to show me everything. I went straight to the King and told him. He was stupefied and fell prostrate at my feet, paid me honour and ordered that an offering and incense be presented to me. I was very quick to give the glory to God, I assure you. Not only that, the King lavished many gifts on me, made me ruler over the entire province of Babylon and placed me in charge of all its wise men.

JOSEPH ISN'T THE ONLY ONE (2)

So there I was, living "high on the hog" so to speak, just like Joseph. But I don't think Joseph had to face what came next. It all happened because, In my view, the king was unstable. He decided to build an image ninety feet high and ordered everyone to fall down and worship it whenever the music sounded. If you didn't comply you would be thrown into a blazing furnace. I was only too well aware that Israel and Judah had been taken into exile and disgrace for worshipping gods other than the true and living God. So there was no way I was going to compound the offence by worshipping a lump of gold that God gave us in the first place, even if it meant the loss of my life. So I refused and so did my three Jewish companions. All those astrologers, whose noses I had put out of joint when God gave me the interpretation of the King's dream, were only too quick to denounce us. However, they knew that the king valued my services too highly to throw me into the fire, so they denounced only my three companions.

The king, furious with rage, summoned them and gave them one more chance to worship his statue, which they turned down. He then summoned the strongest soldiers in his army and had them build up the furnace to such a heat that when the three got thrown into it the guards perished in the flames. Well, the king was watching to see what would happen. To his utter astonishment he could see four men walking around in the fire, one of whom he described as looking like "a son of the gods". So he calls them all out of the fire and out the three emerge – no sign of the fourth. Everyone crowds round to examine them but there's absolutely no trace of any scorching or singeing or smell of fire. The king is mightily impressed and issues a decree that no-one is to say anything against the God of the three. If they do they will be cut into pieces and their houses turned into rubble. Who were these three? Shadrach, Meshach and Abednego.

Quite frankly, dealing with the king is proving terrifying. One minute he's all charm and kindness; the next he's gratuitously cruel. So when he tells me he's had another dream I really don't want to get involved but I daren't not. So he tells me about this ghastly dream and I have to interpret it. It's awful. I have to tell the king that he's going to go mad and that this madness is going to last seven years until he acknowledges the Sovereign God. But if he renounces his sins and starts being kind to the oppressed perhaps this disaster can be averted.

JOSEPH ISN'T THE ONLY ONE (3)

A year later Nebuchadnezzar is looking out over Babylon and admiring all his construction done "by my mighty power and for the glory of my majesty". Guess what happens. He goes mad. The Bible tells it more graphically than I can *"He was driven away from people and ate grass like cattle. His body was drenched with the dew of heaven until his hair grew like the feathers of an eagle and his nails like the claws of a bird."* Pathetic, really. However, after the appointed time his sanity was restored and he gave glory to God. Quite an important message for us in there, don't you think?

Anyway, I'm still around when Belshazzar, his son, ascends to the throne. He's a dreadful man. He holds a banquet and uses the goblets that had been used in the temple at Jerusalem, not just to drink from, which is bad enough, but also give praise to gods of gold, silver, bronze, iron, wood and stone. You would think he would have learned from what happened to Nebuchadnezzar. As they're drinking, a human hand appears and writes on the wall. I told you I could match Joseph when it comes to storytelling. The message on the wall is "Mene, mene, tekel, parsin." Nobody can translate it, not even the astrologers and wise men, so they're all sitting there looking stunned and scared to death, when the queen comes in to see what's disturbing everyone. She remembers that I used to interpret for Nebuchadnezzar and urges the king to call for me.

Well, you need to know that I am appalled at the way the King has abused his position in using goblets made for the worship of God to worship his own stupid gods that don't even exist. So when I arrive I use the opportunity to point out that Belshazzar has done a very foolish thing in setting himself up against the Lord of Heaven instead of honouring him. He will now reap the consequences. This is what I told him:

"*Mene: God has numbered the days and brought them to an end.*"
"*Tekel: You have been weighed on the scales and found wanting.*"
"*Peresh: Your kingdom is divided and given to the Medes and Persians.*"

Although I didn't want any of it, Belshazzar commands that I be clothed in purple, given a gold chain to go round my neck and proclaimed the third highest ruler in the kingdom. (I know that Joseph was promoted to number two in Egypt whereas I was only promoted to number three in Babylon but I haven't finished my story yet.) There wasn't much point to all this promotion because, that very night, Belshazzar was slain and Darius the Mede took over the kingdom, at the ripe old age of sixty-two.

JOSEPH ISN'T THE ONLY ONE (4)

Darius and I got on pretty well but he did have a weakness for his own importance. That caused the next "event" in my story. Darius intended to promote me to become the administrator over the whole kingdom. Needless to say, this got up the noses, yet again, of the other administrators and satraps who tried to find grounds to charge me for maladministration. As they couldn't find anything to hold against me, they decided to appeal to the King's vanity. They did this by persuading him to issue an edict that anyone who prayed to any god or man other than him should be thrown into the lions' den. They knew that I wouldn't pray to anyone except my God so they thought they had me.

That evening the king gave the order and I got thrown into the lions' den. I thought the end had come and was prepared for it. When I landed in the den and picked myself up there were the lions coming towards me and looking mighty hungry. But then an astonishing thing happened. An angel appeared. I expect you know about angels. They're not the sort of person you want to meet on a dark night if you're up to mischief. This one looked really scary and had a flaming sword. He touched the lions on their mouths and they, the mouths that is, stayed shut all night. In fact, all they could do was lie as far away from me as they could get and wimper.

Well, the king was pretty distraught that he had to throw me into the den in the first place so, at first light, he was down there checking to see if there was any hope for me. I was able to assure him that all was well and that God had rescued me. He had me lifted out of the den and then ordered that those who had accused me, together with their families should be thrown in instead. No sooner was this done that the lions killed them all. The net result of all this was that I prospered during the reigns of both Darius and Cyrus, his successor.

I don't know about you but I think that's a story that can more than hold its own with that of Joseph. And if that wasn't enough, God gave me some monumental visions and dreams that you will find in the latter half of my book in the Old Testament. Even today, 2,500 years later, experts are still trying to interpret precisely what they meant.

ARE YOU GOOD AT LEARNING THE HARD WAY?

Daniel

I am, me, Nebuchadnezzar

You can't imagine how powerful I was. I ruled over a mighty empire, with a vast number of provinces. I restored Babylon to great majesty, wealth and luxury.

Do you recall the Hanging Gardens of Babylon? One of the seven ancient wonders of the world? That was me. In the second year of my reign I had a dream. Only one person could tell me what the dream was about and that was Daniel, one of the Israelite exiles I had appointed to my administration. I was astonished at the accuracy of his account of my dream and its interpretation. I noted that it was his God who revealed this to him. So I fell on my knees and worshipped him and his God.

It didn't last. I was too busy to bow down to an Israelite God every day. I was having a magnificent statue built. Everyone had to bow down to it. Unfortunately, some astrologers came forward and told me Daniel and his Israelite friends refused to do so. I had to act. Into the fiery furnace they went – and came out again, totally unsinged. Yet again I gave glory to the God of the Israelites at this extraordinary outcome.

Yet again, it didn't last. Then I had another dream which, quite frankly, terrified me. It terrified Daniel as well. As usual, he was the only one who could interpret it. He said his God gave him the interpretation. I was going to go mad, live like the wild animals, eat grass like cattle and be drenched with dew. What was worse, this was going to last seven years. Daniel added in some advice of his own. If I acknowledged the God of Heaven, renounced my sins by doing what was right and was kind to the oppressed, then my prosperity might continue and this awful fate might be avoided.

Did I listen? No. I didn't. I was preoccupied with my own importance. I can still remember the words that triggered the dream's fulfilment: "Is not this the great Babylon I have built as the royal residence, by my mighty power and for the glory of my majesty?" Out into the wilds I went, for seven years.

Let me tell you what I learned – to praise and exalt and glorify the King of Heaven, because everything he does is right and just. And those who walk in pride he is able to humble.

Please don't learn the hard way.

MY NAME'S HOSEA AND I'M A PROPHET

Hosea

Yes, my name's Hosea and I'm a prophet but, frankly, I wish I wasn't. Let me explain.

I prophesied for many years. During that time Israel was a total disgrace. We had six kings within 25 years. Four of them were murdered by their successors. One was captured in battle and only one was succeeded by his son. Worse, there was a complete disregard of the God who brought us out of Egypt, gave us our land and promised to prosper and defend us if we would honour and worship only him. I won't go into all the details of what went wrong. Suffice it to say that the whole enterprise of Israel and Judah ended in death, destruction and exile.

Well, of course I went round warning everyone of the trouble they were storing up. I felt rather like the man with the sandwich board - although sandwiches hadn't been invented then. Nobody liked me; nobody listened to me. I can't say I was happy pronouncing death and destruction unless we turned back to God – but I did it. What I hadn't appreciated at the start of my roughly 38 years of prophesying was that God would actually want me to live out the allegory of his relationship with Israel.

To start with I couldn't believe it. "You want me to do what? Marry an adulteress?" I had to check because it was something totally against my upbringing. Anyway, I married Gomer and she gave me three children. So far so good but then God told me how I had to name them – "Jezreel" because he would inflict punishment for the massacre at Jezreel; "Lo-Ruhamah" because He would no longer show love to Israel and "Lo-Amni" because Israel was no longer his people and he was no longer their God.

If that wasn't bad enough, Gomer went off with someone else and ended up as a slave. She duly became the adulteress God had told me she would be. To make matters worse God then instructed me to love her again *though she is loved by another and is an adulteress. Love her as the Lord loves the Israelites though they turn to other gods.* So I bought Gomer back for fifteen shekels of silver and about a homer and a lethek of barley. Then I told her "…you must not be a prostitute or be intimate with any man and I will live with you."

Do you see now why I wish I wasn't a prophet?

AN INTERVIEW WITH EZEKIEL

Ezekiel

I: "If I can get straight into things, Ezekiel? How did you become a prophet?"

E: "I wasn't looking to become one. I was one of the exiles taken to Babylon in 597BC. I'd been there five years when I saw the most extraordinary and terrifying vision. It was God. He told me he was sending me to the Israelites who needed to hear what I was to be given to say."

I: "And what was that? How did that work out?"

E: "A hand reached out to me. In it was a scroll with words written on it. I had to eat it. It tasted like honey."

I: "So did you start prophesying straight away?"

E: "It was after seven days that I got my orders. If I didn't speak out I would die."

I : "How did you know it was God speaking to you?"

E: "Because I could see him."

I : "What was the first thing you had to do?"

E: "Draw a plan of Jerusalem. Then lay siege to it by building a ramp and putting in place battering rams and camps all around it. Then, symbolically, I had to bear the sins of Israel and Judah. That meant lying on my left side for the sins of Israel 390 days and on my right for the sins of Judah 40 days.

I was given a daily ration of food which I had to cook over cow dung."

I: "Wasn't that rather extreme?"

E: "I wasn't about to argue. I can't tell you how angry God was. He planned the destruction of Jerusalem. His messages were so drastic that people died whilst listening to them. He took me to Jerusalem to see the awful things going on there."

I: "So what was the worst thing that you had to endure?"

E: "The death of my wife. God declared that the children of the exiles left behind in Jerusalem would fall by the sword. They would die as my wife died. I wasn't allowed to mourn her; I could only groan quietly."

I: "What a terrible commission you had."

E: "God did show me that he would restore Israel. He showed me the new temple area, how the land would be divided amongst the tribes and that the glory would return to the temple where God would live for ever.

I: "Why didn't you just say "Please find someone else to be your prophet?"

E: "When God speaks you argue at your peril."

I: "Thank you."

GOD IS AMAZING

Esther

Esther: "Now, what was it you wanted to ask me?"

Journalist: "I'm researching our nation's exile. I've been told that you were a key figure for a time. I wondered if you can you tell me anything about that?"

E: "Indeed I can. I remember it as if it was yesterday. I didn't always look like this you know. I was a real beauty in my day, though I say so myself. For some reason, the King of Persia got fed up with his wife and divorced her. Then he ordered a search to be made of all 127 provinces to find a suitable replacement. I was one of those chosen for the final stage. Then, to my amazement, the King decided I should become his new wife. He didn't know I was a Jewess.

Everything was lovely for a while but then I discovered that a rising star at court, one Haman, had it in mind to destroy us Jews and even persuaded the King to issue a decree to that effect. You can imagine the anxiety and panic that ensued. My uncle, Mordecai, got word to me that I should go in to see the King and plead for our lives. I pointed out to him that if I was to go in to the King unannounced and he wasn't happy about it I would pay with my life. That didn't impress Mordecai one bit. He told me that God would save his people and if it wasn't through me it would be through someone else, in which case I and my family would perish.

So, I told Mordecai to get everyone to fast and pray for three days, dressed myself up in my finest robes and went in to the King. I can tell you my heart was pounding so hard I thought it would seize up. Well, he welcomed me in so I invited him and the wretched Haman to a banquet. I there explained the whole plot to the King. I don't think the King had fully understood what he had previously agreed to. He was furious and went out into the garden to get over his anger, leaving Haman to fall all over me begging for mercy.

The king came back in to discover what he thought was Haman assaulting me. Well that was curtains for Haman. He got hung and we Jews were authorised to attack all those who had intended to attack us. We were safe. God is amazing.

MORDECAI'S STORY

Esther

You've heard Esther's story but you haven't heard mine, which means you haven't heard the half of it. Who would have thought that God would use an old man and a young maiden to deliver his people from death? In a way, you could say Esther and I were forerunners of Simeon and Mary. This is how it all worked out from my point of view.

I was gutted when the King's emissaries took Esther away to be one of the select group of virgins from whom King Xerxes would choose his next queen. Frankly, I was even more gutted when Esther was actually chosen to be the next queen but the more I thought about it the more I thought this might work out well for us Jews, although I told her not to disclose the fact that she was a Jewess. In any case, I took up a position close to the harem quarters and stayed in touch with Esther.

As a result of my sitting at the King's gate I overheard the plotting of a conspiracy to assassinate the King. I passed the information to Esther, who passed it to the king whilst giving me the credit. The information was investigated and found to be accurate. My actions and the subsequent foiling of the plot were recorded in the King's annals. It was shortly afterwards that Haman, one of the king's favourites, plotted to destroy all of the Israelites, starting with me, simply because I would not bow down to him. He even built a gallows, seventy five feet high to hang me on. The night before the hanging the

King couldn't sleep so he ordered his annals to be read to him, including the story of how I foiled the conspiracy. On discovering that nothing had been done to reward me the king made Haman of all people conduct me round Susa, with me wearing a crown and a set of the king's robes and Haman telling everyone "This is what is done for the man the king delights to honour."

Well, you know the rest of the story because Esther told you. But what you don't know is that the king raised me to become second in rank to himself with authority over the 127 provinces that stretched from India to Cush. Yes, I was up there with Joseph who was second only to Pharaoh and Daniel who was appointed by King Darius ruler over the entire province of Babylon. With God nothing is impossible.

CAN WE LEARN ANYTHING FROM THE OLD TESTAMENT?

At the heart of the Old Testament is the story of Israel – its formation, its growth in power and territory and its decline and exile. It's rather a sad story, although parts of it are pleasant.

Way back then, God spoke to people directly. One of them was Abraham. God promised Abraham that he would be the father of a nation so large that it would be uncountable. That was Israel. It would be through Israel that all other nations would be blessed. This was how God would show his love for us all. In return God asked the people of Israel to love him and each other.

What we see in the Old Testament is the story of what happened when Israel obeyed God and what happened when it didn't. The zenith of Israel's might and power came at the time of Kings David and Solomon. At that time the territory of Israel stretched from the border of Egypt to Damascus and beyond. Every nation, except Egypt – a broken reed - bordering Israel paid tribute or acknowledged Israel's authority. According to a census ordered by King David, the fighting manpower of Israel in his time amounted to 1.3 million men. Add in women, children and the old and infirm and the population must have exceeded 2 million.

After the reigns of Kings David and Solomon things slowly went from bad to worse. The second book of Kings in the Old Testament provides us with a litany of disaster. This is how a typical reign is recorded in that book: *"In the thirty-seventh year of Joash, king of Judah, Jehoash son of Jehoahaz became king of Israel* (at that time Israel had split into two nations – Israel and Judah). *He did evil in the eyes of the Lord and did not turn away from the sins of Jeroboam son of Nebat which he had caused Israel to commit."* Those sins included the worship of golden calves in place of God. By that time, Israel's army had shrunk from an impressive 800,000 to a meagre 50 horsemen, 10 chariots and 10,000 foot soldiers.

So what's the lesson we can learn from this sorry saga in the Old Testament? In short, if we as a nation love and honour God and him alone then we will prosper. However, if our nation leaves God out of the equation don't be surprised if over time our power and influence evaporate. What do you think is happening?

WHEN GOD SPEAKS...

Ezra 1

Was it a combination of God and Daniel that provided the impetus for the Emperor Cyrus to issue a decree in 538BC? It was the first year of his reign and the seventieth year of the exile of the Jews. The decree permitted the Jewish exiles to return to Israel, taking with them the artefacts that had been stripped from the temple before it was destroyed. After all, Cyrus became king only three years after the fateful night that saw the hand of God appear and the writing on the wall foretelling the downfall of King Belshazzar. God used Daniel to interpret that writing. Was it a desire on the part of Cyrus to get rid of the Jews whose God had caused so much trouble? Why else, if you are the ruler of all the kingdoms of the earth, would you trouble yourself over one tiny little part of that great empire? It doesn't appear that way from the wording of the decree but then, of course, a ruler of all the kingdoms of the earth wouldn't allow an emotion such as fear to colour a decree, would he?

"The Lord, the God of Heaven, has given me all the kingdoms of the earth and he has appointed me to build a temple for him at Jerusalem in Judah. Anyone of his people among you – may his God be with him - and let him go up to Jerusalem in Judah and build the temple of the Lord, the God of Israel, the God who is in Jerusalem..."

Have you ever felt that you were part of something much bigger than you anticipated? Something you thought you were in control of but realised later how fortunate you were that things worked out the way they did? Did Cyrus know, when he issued his decree, of the prophecy that Jeremiah uttered all those years previously? A prophecy terrible for both Israel and Babylon?

"I will summon all the peoples of the north and my servant Nebuchadnezzar, king of Babylon, and I will bring them against this land and its inhabitants and against all the surrounding nations. I will completely destroy them and make them an object of horror and scorn, an everlasting ruin....This whole country will become a desolate wasteland, and these nations will serve the king of Babylon for seventy years. But when the seventy years are fulfilled, I will punish the king of Babylon...and the land of the Babylonians...and will make it desolate for ever."

When God speaks, listen.

NOTHING BUT TROUBLE

Ezra

I didn't ask for this job. But you don't argue with an emperor who can terminate your life with a flick of his finger. So here I am, Tattenai, governor of the Trans-Euphrates region. It's a mess. By the time everyone from Tilgath-Pileser to Nebuchadnezzar and their armies had trampled over the region there were piles of rubble everywhere. And the exiles! Lowest of the low from other parts of the Persian empire. There were, however, opportunities to better myself and my circumstances. I was, after all, responsible for tax collection and deciding conflicts. So I wasn't where I would have liked to be but things could have been worse. That was the situation until they turned up.

Who are they? Them, the Jews. One day they weren't here, the next there were over 40,000 of them. They just settled down in their original homes, totally ignoring me and my officials. There were just too many of them for me to kick them out again. In any case, they said they had permission from King Cyrus, so what could I do? If they'd just got on with their lives and not caused any disturbances I would have been a happy man but, no, they had to go and start rebuilding their temple in Jerusalem. Well, we all know what that means, a focus for revolt. So I wrote to the king about it. It was Artaxerxes by then. Alright, I did exaggerate and say they were rebuilding the city walls and foundations. But they would have got round to that in due course

The king had a search made of the archives and discovered that the Jews were indeed a rebellious and unruly lot. So he ordered that building work should stop immediately. I took a strong force of men to Jerusalem and forced the them to stop. Life returned to a reasonably satisfactory standard and continued for a number of years when, blow me down, if the Jews didn't start rebuilding the temple again. I asked them on what authority they were doing so and they quoted from the decree by King Cyrus. I again wrote to the King but this time I added in the response from the Jews.

The king again had a search made of the archives and found out that there had indeed been a decree. So he wrote and told me not to interfere. Not only that, I had to pay their expenses! Things quietened down after that, until Nehemiah turned up.....

A BUILDING PROJECT

Nehemiah

You don't come into the presence of the king looking sad. You could be thrown out or, worse, jailed or executed. I couldn't help it. The king noticed. He wanted to know why. I told him about Jerusalem's destruction. I can't tell you how scared I was. The king was silent for a moment and then, praise God, asked me what I wanted. He must have been in a very good mood. I think it might have had something to do with the fact that he had the queen sitting with him. She always cheered him up.

I knew I was still on dangerous ground but something had to be done. So, throwing up a silent prayer I asked the king to release me from my duties so that I could leave to rebuild Jerusalem. I think it pleased the king to see the idea as some sort of project because he asked me how long I would be away and when I would return. I set a time. I also asked for letters to the governor of Trans-Euphrates to provide safe conduct and to Asaph, keeper of the king's forest, for building material. Not only did I get those but I also got an escort of officers and cavalry.

We made quite an impression on the local officials when we arrived. Talk about disturbed! Anyway, I handed over the letters and then went out to inspect the city walls. The reports I'd had turned out to be, if anything, an understatement. The whole city lay in ruins and the gates had been burned to charcoal. It seemed impossible to put it all back together. However, there was no way I was going back to the king without having completed my mission. So I called together all the Jews, priests, nobles, officials, in fact anyone who could turn a hand to helping. I explained why I was there and exhorted them to help.

I got a really positive response. We were able to divide the walls up into sections, allocate them as appropriate and set about the work of rebuilding. Needless to say, we had nothing but mockery and scorn from the local officials to start with. We just ignored that. But when they saw how serious we were and what progress we were making matters got a bit more serious. We had to post guards and every man working on the project carried his weapons. We completed the rebuild in fifty-two days. Not bad for a bunch of exiles.

THIS IS WHY WE NEED JESUS

Nehemiah

It took Nehemiah twelve years to sort out Jerusalem post the exile. He left King Artaxerxes' employ in the twentieth year of the king's reign and returned in the thirty-second. Whilst Nehemiah repaired the walls of Jerusalem in fifty-two days there was a lot else that needed repair.

Poverty was rampant. Fields, vineyards and homes were being mortgaged. Money was being borrowed to pay taxes. Children were being sold into slavery. Usury was being exacted. Intermarriage with other races was happening. Trade was being carried out on the Sabbath. The first fruits of the harvest and family were not being brought for dedication to the Lord.

Nehemiah put all that right. He started in the most sensible place, the Book of the Law of Moses. On the first of the month, our October 8th, Ezra read it to all the assembled Israelites. The reading lasted several days. On October 30th all the Israelites reassembled, fasting and wearing sackcloth with dust on their heads. They acknowledged the sins of their forefathers at some length and bound themselves with an oath and a curse to "follow the Law of God given through Moses and to obey carefully all the laws and decrees of the Lord, our Lord."

Having got the Israelites on the right track Nehemiah felt able to return to Babylon. But his heart remained in Jerusalem so, again with the king's permission, he returned to see how things were going. The first thing he found was that the Levites and singers, who were responsible for the services of the temple had not received the food portions due to them and so had returned to their towns. He put that right. Then he saw men in Judah doing commercial work and bringing the fruits of that work into Jerusalem on the Sabbath. He put a stop to that. Then he noticed that intermarriage had again taken place and that some children could not speak the language of Judah. So he put that right.

What's the point of all this? Quite simply, the Israelites committed themselves to follow the Law but like their forefathers before them, proved unable to do so. It's just not possible. Think New Year's Resolutions. No-one keeps the law in full. But Jesus speaks to our hearts as well as our minds. If your heart is right with God you will want to obey the law, confess your sins when you don't and start out again determined to preserve that healthy relationship with God through Jesus.

HAVE YOU EVER BEEN A FISH?

Jonah

Have you ever been a fish? No? I thought not. I have to laugh when I see you floundering (excuse the pun – flounder? Fish? Get it?) in the sea. Me? One flick of the tail and I can shoot past all of you, even though I'm pretty large. Actually, I'm one of the largest fish in the sea. The minnows scoot off when they see me coming. I have this tremendous trick of opening my mouth wide and scooping up plankton at an amazing rate. It's dead easy for someone as big and powerful as I am.

My favourite fishing region is the Mediterranean, no question, particularly down the east end of the sea. I don't go there often; it gets a bit cramped for someone like me who can cover hundreds of miles at a time. But the plankton down there seem to have a rather nice flavour. If it gets rough I just slip down a few feet to where there's a nice swell that lulls me to sleep.

I'm in the Mediterranean when a terrific storm blows up. I would have taken my usual precautions but it so happened that I was still hungry. So I reckoned I had time for one more fishing foray if I hurried. I wasn't as careful as I usually am. I just shot along at high speed, mouth wide open. Suddenly there was this great clump in my throat and I'd actually swallowed one of you. That gave me a bit of a turn.

I'd never experienced that before so I thought I'd wait a bit before doing anything rash. It wasn't very comfortable. First of all this human kept tickling my stomach. With no arms I couldn't do anything about it and I kept laughing which meant I swallowed water when I didn't mean to. Then he started banging on the sides of my stomach and kicking me. It wasn't long before I knew I had to do something to get rid of him. My first thought was to kill him. So I took to leaping out of the sea and coming down flat with a huge bang. That didn't work. Then I tried to suffocate him by diving as deep as I could go and not breathing. That didn't work. Finally, I swam at enormous speed onto the beach and came to a dead stop with my mouth wide open. He shot out as if from a catapult.

Now what was that all about?

A MESSAGE TO THE ENEMIES OF ISRAEL

Zechariah

Have you heard of Zechariah? Have you read the Old Testament of the Bible? He's in there and has a book all to himself. He lived 500 years before Christ appeared.

Now many of you are hostile to Israel. You resent the fact that the Palestinians have been driven off that land

and want to reinstate them. It's almost in your genes that there will come a day when you will all come together to "drive Israel into the sea". I'm quoting there a President of Iran. The idea of all you nations uniting to destroy Israel is a very heart-warming one for you. Given the chance, you would have no hesitation in killing off every last Jewish man, woman and child. Putting an end to the state and people of Israel in a way of which Hitler would have approved.

Before you do anything further to achieve that end, let me tell you what God revealed to Zechariah.

"The Lord, who stretches out the heavens, who lays the foundation of the earth, and who forms the spirit of man within him, declares: "I am going to make Jerusalem a cup that sends all the surrounding peoples reeling. Judah will be besieged as well as Jerusalem. On that day when all the nations of the earth are gathered against her, I will make Jerusalem an immovable rock for all the nations. All who try to move it will injure themselves. On that day I will strike every horse with panic and its rider with madness," declares the Lord. "I will keep a watchful eye over the house of Judah, but I will blind all the horses of the nations. Then the leaders of Israel will say in their hearts, "The people of Jerusalem are strong because the Lord Almighty is their God.""

Do you see what's written there? You will be fighting against God. Whilst it may appear that initially you are being successful the end result, if you persist in fighting on, is your sure destruction. I could quote more of the same. It's all there in Zechariah, chapter 12.

Verse 9 concludes "On that day I will set out to destroy all the nations that attack Jerusalem."

If, as you maintain, your God is the same as the Jewish God then you will be fighting against your God. Don't do it. There can be only one result. Take this message to heart. Allow Israel to live in peace – or face the consequences. You have been warned.

150 SHARDS OF LIGHT – NEW TESTAMENT

I'VE HEARD QUITE ENOUGH!

Luke 2

Location: District Court Martial Centre, Roman Garrison, Bethlehem
Time: 261030hrs Dec.

President: "Are you IXMCCCXLII Flavius Caligulus Seneca, a soldier of the XXIX legion?"
Flavius: "Yes, sir."
President: "You are charged with deserting your sentry post. How do you plead?"
Flavius: "Guilty but with mitigating circumstances."
President: "Mitigating circumstances? A Roman soldier doesn't need those to explain his actions."
Flavius: "Well, if I could just explain, Sir. I was on sentry duty about 2 miles outside Bethlehem. These shepherds came along and pitched camp about 100 paces from my post, which isn't allowed. So I went over to move them on. I was about 30 paces from them when I got the fright of my life. Hanging in the air about 10 paces up was a ball of light and in this light was the figure of a man, holding a flaming sword.

I fell flat on my face but I could hear what the man was saying. He was telling them to go into Bethlehem where they would find someone called the Messiah. Then, suddenly, he wasn't alone. There were hundreds of them singing "Glory to God in the highest and peace on earth." Then they all disappeared. The shepherds did a bit of jabbering and then shot off towards Bethlehem.

Well, it's not every day you see something like that so, without another thought I was up and after them. They seemed to know exactly where to go. It was a local drinking house with an annex attached. They pushed at the door and went in, leaving the door open. So I looked in and there was this family with a baby in a crib. And that was that. A hand gripped my shoulder and I was arrested by the town patrol sergeant. And that's all I've got to say.

President: I think we've heard quite enough too! When it comes to tall stories, this is about the best I've heard. This trial need proceed no further. Flavius Caligulus Seneca not only are you found guilty of deserting your post, you are also guilty of entering an out of bounds area, of being in possession of a weapon in a native quarter and likely to cause unrest, of being unaccompanied in a native village and of being an out and out liar. You are hereby sentenced to receive 25 lashes of the whip, six months detention and to be posted to the galleys for two years. I doubt if you'll survive that!

Provost, take him away!

LAST WILL AND TESTAMENT?

Luke 3

My Darling Rebecca

Although you can't read now you will be able to one day. So I am sending this letter to your mother for safe keeping.

She will be able to tell you about my life – probably in more detail than I can! We were very close as I had no children of my own. I did marry though. My husband was lovely and I still miss him. We were only married for seven years. I've been on my own for 60 years – that makes me 84. I haven't got much time which is why I am writing to you now. I have something of the utmost importance to share.

Following my husband's death I decided to dedicate my life to God. I began going to the temple in Jerusalem every day. After a while, it seemed as if God wanted to use me in a powerful way because the temple priests recognised that I had the gift of prophecy. They invited me to stay in the temple on a permanent basis, so I could be available at any time to speak into situations as they developed. They gave me a comfortable room and looked after my needs.

It wasn't long afterwards that God spoke to me. It was a message I will never forget. He told me the Christ was coming and I would see him! When you get to school age you will be taught about how the anointed one is going to rescue Israel and restore her to former glory, probably by driving out the Romans, and installing himself as a powerful king. Your teachers will be utterly wrong. I have seen him! He is a babe in arms but he will grow to die an appalling death to pay the price for our sins and put us right with God. He will then ascend to rule over his Kingdom - a kingdom not yet of this world but he will assuredly have one.

His parents brought him to the temple to be dedicated. I went over to help them. That's when I saw the baby. God said to me "Behold, your Christ!" My heart stood still. My mouth was opened and I prophesied with such power as I had never experienced before. His name is Jesus. When you meet him, as you will if you look out for him – follow him. Let him be your King.

Good bye darling Rebecca. May God bless you as he has blessed me.

Your loving great aunt Anna

NO BABY? WHAT A DISGRACE!

Luke 1

The Bible tells us of women who were unable to have children. One example was Sarai, Abram's wife. The Bible describes her as "barren". In her desperation to provide Abram with a son, she persuaded him to sleep with her Egyptian maidservant, Hagar. This unfortunate union produced Ishmael, whose offspring became a nation and a thorn in the side of Israel. Once Hagar realised she was pregnant she despised Sarai. No baby? What a disgrace!

Then there's Hannah. Elkanah had two wives, Hannah and Peninnah. Peninnah had children; Hannah had none. Peninnah kept provoking Hannah in order to irritate her. No baby? What a disgrace! Once, whilst the family was at the temple, Hannah made a vow. *"O Lord Almighty, if you will only look upon your servant's misery and remember me…and give your servant a son, then I will give him to the Lord for all the days of his life…"* In the beautiful language of the Bible we read that they went home and *"Elkanah lay with Hannah, his wife, and the Lord remembered her. So, in course of time Hannah conceived and gave birth to a son. She named him Samuel, saying "Because I asked the Lord for him."* Samuel became probably the greatest judge that Israel ever had.

But why was "barrenness" such a disgrace and deemed to be some sort of punishment from the Lord? I think the answer lies in the need to produce many children because child mortality was probably very high. Similarly, life expectancy was probably very low due to the lack of modern medicines and the scourge of plagues, famines, floods and so on. The absence of any sort of birth control meant that the conception of a child would likely be an annual event unlike our modern society, where conception occurs mainly on demand. A journey through the local village would probably reveal a large number of pregnant women. One who was barren in such a circumstance would almost certainly feel that God had deserted her.

That brings us to the conception of John the Baptist. His parents were Zechariah and Elizabeth. *"They were* *upright in the sight of God, observing all the Lord's commandments and regulations blamelessly. But they had no children, because Elizabeth was barren."*No baby? What a disgrace! An angel visits Zechariah and tells him that Elizabeth will bear him a son. Sure enough, that's exactly what happens. Elizabeth rejoices and says *"The Lord has done this for me....He has taken away my disgrace among the people."*

DID YOU BRING ANYTHING TO EAT?

Luke 3

I'm John. People call me John the Baptist. Yes, I baptised a lot of people. Thanks for visiting me in this prison. Why am I here? It's a long story but then I'm not going anywhere.

An angel told my father he would have a son. I would be a joy and a delight to him and many would rejoice because of my birth. I would be filled with the Holy Spirit. I would be great in the sight of the Lord. I would bring back many people to the Lord their God, and make ready a people prepared for the Lord.

I didn't understand any of it. However, as I grew I increasingly had this desire to take myself off somewhere so I could be close to God without interruption. So I went into the desert and eked out an existence living off the land or passing nomads. I began to understand my mission. Isaiah prophesied it. *"Prepare the way for the Lord, make straight paths for him.....and all mankind will see God's salvation."*

I said "Alright God. I'll preach that but I'm leaving the end result to you." So I started preaching and God brought the people. More and more came to listen. It wasn't a comfortable message. On several occasions I even called them a brood of vipers. I started baptising them but then, to my horror, they started thinking that I might be the Messiah. I wasted no time putting them straight.

"I baptise you with water. But one more powerful than I will come, the thongs of whose sandals I am not worthy to untie. He will baptise you with the Holy Spirit and with fire."

When Jesus came along I knew my mission was virtually complete. However, God told me to tell people how they should live. Unfortunately, someone asked me about Herod. I knew that if I didn't comment my ministry would be undermined. So I spoke out.

You know that Herod had married Herodias, even though she was already married to his brother! He also had most of his family executed. I attacked him for that. So he put me in this prison. A lot of my disciples left me. I hadn't heard from God for some time. I even sent word to Jesus asking him to confirm that he really was the Son of God, which he did.

So, here I am, languishing in this prison but, you know what? I'm happy. Now, did you bring anything to eat?

WHAT DOES JESUS HAVE THAT WE DON'T?

Luke 5

Luke tells us that Jesus *"grew and became strong; he was filled with wisdom and the grace of God was upon him."* Luke goes on to tell us that, at the age of twelve, Jesus was found amongst the teachers at the temple (in Jerusalem) amazing them with his understanding. Now this is extraordinary! How many mothers reading this article would describe any of their young children as being full of wisdom?

So what was it that Jesus possessed that made him stand out amongst his peers? To make people do things that no-one in their apparently right mind would do? Take Peter, for example. Here was a fisherman who knew all about hardship. What fisherman doesn't - fishing at night when everyone else is in bed, partying or enjoying one another's company, enduring the uncertainties of Galilean weather without the benefit of a weather forecast or an outboard motor? Yet, at the end of a hard night's fishing when he and his companions had caught absolutely nothing and had returned home no doubt exhausted, fed up and looking forward to their beds, Jesus tells Peter to go fishing again and he does. He doesn't even know Jesus yet he obeys him. But that's only the start of an amazing story.

Peter and his companions then catch so many fish that their nets begin to break and they have to call on their partners to help them bring the fish ashore. Did you know that Galilean dried fish was a delicacy in Roman times? Such an enormous catch would have profited Peter hugely. But what then follows should make you sit up. What would you have expected Peter to say? "How on earth did you know where the fish were?" "Why did you do that?" "Who are you?" No, this rough, tough man of the sea falls in front of Jesus and, scared to death, says *"Go away from me Lord, I am a sinful man."*

Jesus then says to Peter *"Don't be afraid. From now on you will catch men."* Whereupon Peter and his companions pull their boats up on shore, leave that huge catch of fish – in fact leave everything - and follow Jesus. Peter gave up a very healthy income and way of life to follow someone he didn't even know. Don't you get the feeling that here is someone who is so special and worthy of our interest that he might be worth spending some time on? I do.

WHY ON EARTH CHOOSE A TAX COLLECTOR?

Luke 5 and 19

We don't know very much from the Gospels about the first disciples. They surface every now and then, usually to demonstrate that they had got hold of the wrong end of the stick. So how did Jesus choose them to become part of his team?

It's quite easy to understand why he chose fishermen – Peter, Andrew, James and John. From fishing to catch fish they moved on to fishing for men. Jesus' words, not mine. Simon and Judas were possibly political activists.

Nathaniel was a "true Israelite". But why Matthew (aka Levi)? He was a tax collector.

Tax collectors were Jews who collected taxes from fellow Jews on behalf of the Romans. They made their living by charging more than was strictly required. It's worth thinking about. If you have the mighty arm of the Roman governor and his military force to back you up, there's not much chance that taxpayers are going to argue with you. But they could hate you. The scope for abusing your power to raise taxes was immense. Tax collectors could and probably did become very wealthy. Matthew certainly did. No sooner did Jesus call him to follow than we find him hosting a dinner for Jesus in his mansion. "*While Jesus was having dinner at Levi's house, <u>many </u>tax collectors and sinners were eating with him and his disciples, for there were many who followed him.*" "Hello darling. I'm home and I've brought 30 or 40 people with me. Can we rustle up some dinner for them?"

Then there was the curious story of Zacchaeus. The Bible tells us that he was a Chief Tax Collector. It mentions that he was wealthy – very wealthy in my view. Because he's short, he climbs a tree the better to see Jesus. His contact with Jesus leads him to immediately repent of past behaviour. So Zacchaeus tells Jesus "*If I have cheated anybody out of anything I will pay back four times the amount....*" If? If? What a curious conditional beginning. If he hasn't cheated anyone then he doesn't need to say it. He knows he has cheated them. That's how he became wealthy. So it's not a case of "If". However, Jesus knows that his remorse is sincere and announces *"Today salvation has come to this house.... for the Son of Man came to save what was lost."*

I think the message here is that, no matter what your background, Jesus can use you if you are willing to let him. Are you?

IS THIS A CHANCE TO MAKE SOME MONEY?

Matthew 5

I'm really disappointed. Who am I? Abraham. Not the Abraham you read about in the Bible. Not that one. No, I'm living in an Israel that's under Roman occupation. I really don't mind them being here. I've done well out of them. Well enough for me and my family to be living in the largest house in the village. And we've got a holiday home down by the River Jordan. Life is pretty good really. Of course I attend the local synagogue and, of course, I've heard about the Messiah. We're all waiting for him to come along, throw the Romans out and establish his own kingdom. Although I'm a bit of a chancer I expect I'll still do pretty well under his regime.

So why am I disappointed? Because of that stupid brother of mine, Josiah. He lives in Galilee but drops in occasionally. He came bursting in on me while I was doing my monthly accounting, sending carefully stacked piles of coins flying and told me he'd heard that the Messiah had arrived and was coming my way. "How do you know he's the Messiah?" I asked, not unreasonably I thought. "Because he's been travelling around Galilee teaching in all the synagogues and preaching the good news about his kingdom," said Josiah. "Look," I said, "anyone can do that. What's he done to back up what he's talking about?" "That's just the point," answered Josiah, "He's been healing anyone and everyone - people suffering from diseases, from severe pain, the demon-possessed, those having seizures and the paralysed - everyone. It's totally amazing!"

I thought I'd better check this out. If there's going to be a change of regime, I want to be in at the start. That's where the best opportunities to make money usually are. "How do I get to meet this guy?" I asked Josiah. "You can't miss him." He replied, "He's just up the road on the hill outside the village with a huge crowd. Come on, let's go!" So I went and I came home disappointed. You know what he said? *"Blessed are the poor in spirit , those who mourn, the meek, those who hunger and thirst after righteousness, the merciful, the pure in heart, the peacemakers and those who are persecuted."* Losers all of them. Well, that's not me. And then, to top it all off, he made it clear that his kingdom is not of this world anyway. Now what use it that to me?

ARE YOU TAKING THIS IN?

Matthew 5

Saul: "I was really taken by this chap Jesus. He's out for the downtrodden and the poor. I like that. I like to help where I can. We've got something in common. I left halfway through, so would you mind bringing me up to date on the rest of his talk?"

Jacob: "Knowing you as I do, Saul, I'm not sure how you're going to like this. Basically, Jesus laid out some obligations if you're to follow him."

S: "Oh, come on! They can't be too bad, surely?"

J: "Well, anyone who says "You fool!" is in danger of the fire of hell."

S: "What?! I'm always calling that slave of mine a fool. I don't know why I keep him. Anyway, what else?"

J: "You're not supposed to commit adultery."

S: "Well, I haven't, at least not yet, although I can't keep my eyes off the daughter of that family that's just moved in. She's a real beauty."

J: "Jesus said anyone who looks at a woman lustfully has already committed adultery with her in his heart."

S: "I'm afraid I'm going to have trouble with that one. Any more?"

J: "Yes, If you decide to divorce your wife because of that girl next door you cause her to become an adulteress, if she gets involved with anyone else."

S: "So now Jesus is telling me I can't divorce any more wives? Preposterous!"

J: "There's more. You've got to stop swearing. Just say "Yes" or "No"

S: "I'm not sure I could live with that one."

J: "Jesus also said, if someone strikes you turn the other cheek."

S: "What? I didn't get to where I am by allowing everyone to walk all over me."

J: "You've also got to love your enemies and pray for those who persecute you."

S: "This is getting ridiculous. Love your enemies? Fat chance."

J: "When you give to the needy, don't do it with a fanfare of trumpets in the synagogue."

S: "But how else am I going to let everyone know I'm giving more to the poor than they do?"

J: "Jesus also said don't store up treasures on earth because that's where your heart will be. You can't serve God and money."

S: "I've heard enough! I can't meet all those obligations. And I don't see how anyone else can."

J: "That's the whole point. If your heart's right you'll want to try. Where you fall short trying Jesus will stand in the gap."

S: "Hmmm."

WHAT WAS GOING ON HERE?

John 3

I sometimes wonder whether we haven't got hold of the wrong end of the stick. The background to this story from the pages of John's Gospel concerns a man named Nicodemus. He's a member of the Pharisees. Now Pharisees were upholders of the law of Moses and saw to it that everyone else upheld it too, in minutest detail. When Jesus came along and started preaching, his message differed from that of the Pharisees. So here we have the story of how Nicodemus seeks to understand better what Jesus' message is.

There are certain things that Nicodemus knows about Jesus. He knows he is a Rabbi or teacher because that's how he addresses him. He says he knows Jesus comes from God because of the miraculous signs Jesus is doing. But he doesn't ask Jesus straight out what he stands for. So Jesus brushes aside all the flattery and tells Nicodemus straight out what Nicodemus really wants to know, *"No-one can see the Kingdom of God unless he is born again."*

Now, there are certain things we know about Nicodemus. Besides being a Pharisee, he is a teacher of Israel. That puts him in a position of power and influence. Also, he doesn't understand in the slightest what Jesus is telling him. But the most significant thing is that he comes to Jesus at night. Why? The conventional view is that he probably didn't want his fellow Pharisees to know that he was meeting with Jesus.

But I wonder if that's right. Why, for instance, does Jesus spend so much time and effort in explaining to Nicodemus the truth of what he, Jesus, is preaching? Why does Nicodemus get such a special mention? I think it's because he was sent to this meeting by the Pharisees. It wasn't them he didn't want to find out what he was doing. It was the ordinary people. I mean think about it. Jesus has burst onto the scene in an amazing way. The Pharisees need to find out what's going on but don't want to show the people that they are having talks with this strange person. What would that do to their credibility?

So Jesus tells Nicodemus *"God so loved the world that he gave his one and only son that whosoever believed in him should not perish but have eternal life."* Whilst Nicodemus might have taken these words to heart, it is clear that the rest of the Pharisees didn't. I think they had their chance. The rest is history.

I WAS IN THE SYNAGOGUE WHEN IT HAPPENED

Luke 4

It had started out as another hot day in Nazareth. We all plodded our way to the synagogue and took our usual seats. Jacob Asher was a bit put out because his seat was already taken. You know how fussy some people can get about that. Thing is, Jacob's getting on a bit and thought he was entitled to some respect which, of course, included having his seat in the front row of the synagogue. He didn't get anywhere, because the President made it clear that the visitor would take precedence.

Well, you couldn't actually call him a "visitor". I mean we all knew Jesus, Joseph's so-called son. He hadn't been around for some time. This was his first visit for months. But we had heard some strange stories about him – healings, preaching, teaching. So the place was packed out. And there he sat, looking calm and ignoring the disturbance being caused by Jacob.

When the time came for the reading of the scroll, the President handed it to Jesus. Now you know that in our synagogue we were reading our way through Isaiah. So it was Isaiah's scroll that got handed to Jesus but he didn't pick up where the last reader left off. He unrolled the scroll until he got to a really significant part and then he read that. It's so relevant to what I am going to tell you that I'm setting it out here so that you understand.

"The Spirit of the Lord is on me, because he has anointed me to preach good news to the poor. He has sent me to

proclaim freedom for the prisoners and recovery of sight for the blind, to release the oppressed, to proclaim the year of the Lord's favour."

Well, we'd heard all that before. It's about the Messiah for whom we were waiting and would probably go on waiting for another thousand years or so. It wasn't the reading that caused the riot. It was what happened next. Jesus sat down again, in Jacob's seat, and said: "Today, this scripture is fulfilled in your hearing." He was telling us that he was the Messiah! If you'll forgive the expression, all hell broke loose, particularly when he told us we couldn't understand. In a fury, we decided to throw him off the cliff for such a terrible blasphemy. I don't know how but he calmly walked through the crowd and went on his way. He couldn't have been the Messiah.............. could he?

ALL FOR A HERD OF PIGS

Mark 5

The two swineherds came into my office. They were supposed to be looking after the herd of pigs we'd spent years building up. "We were doing our job when this boat comes ashore and the occupants start walking up the track near the cave where the crazy, demon-possessed man lives. Sure enough, as they approach the cave the man comes rushing out. I thought he would do what he usually did which is to attack anyone foolish enough to stray near him. So we wandered over to enjoy the sport. However, as he reached the group of men, he stopped.

We distinctly heard him, as he was shouting, "What do you want with me, Son of God? Have you come to torture me before the appointed time?" Now what sort of greeting was that? Crazy alright! I can tell you both of us were startled. Son of God? What did that mean? So what do you think the leader of the group said?" "How on earth do I know?" I snarled. "I wasn't there, you were. Now get on with it and tell me what's happened."

"We almost forgot the most important part of the story – at least, important from our point of view. The next thing you know the crazy man is on his knees in front of the group leader and the demons are begging, "If you drive us out, send us into the herd of pigs." No! No! We screamed but to no avail. The group leader just says one word, "Go!" The next thing you know the herd is getting excited and rushing around all over the place then, without a moment's hesitation, they plunge over the cliff edge. The whole lot of them! We rush over to see if there are any pigs that can be rescued but they're all dead."

"That's the most ridiculous story I've ever heard." I said. "Are you sure you haven't been drinking?" "Go and see for yourselves, if you don't believe us" replied the swineherds. So we did and it was just as they had described it. Well, we weren't going to stand for that! "Please go away . Get out of here before you do any more damage to us." We all pleaded with the group and they left.

The next thing we hear is that this group are going around the region healing everyone who needs healing, with the exception of our town. What fools we were and all for a herd of pigs.

JESUS DOESN'T DO BLACK AND WHITE

John 2

Did you know in Jesus' time, wedding celebrations could last up to a week? Imagine catering food and drink for a whole week! It's not surprising that the host offers the best wines at the start when everyone's sober. When that runs out, after a few days, I don't suppose too many guests notice the poorer quality of what's left. Now, imagine that the inferior wine also runs out. How would you like everyone in your village to know you as the person whose marriage celebration was marred by the guests having to drink water?

So, when the wedding host starts waving his hands in despair Mary, Jesus' mother, takes note. Now she has been keeping a careful eye on her son as he grows up. What mother doesn't? But Mary's eye is on the extraordinary things that Jesus does and says – and what others say about him. She knows she has a very unusual son – one she believes will handle this situation. So she says to him *"They have no more wine."* Unspoken is the question "What can you do about it?" When Jesus demurs, perhaps thinking "my power to perform miracles should not be wasted on a group of people who have already drunk too much", his mother lands him in it by saying to the servants *"Do whatever he tells you."*

I think at this point Jesus sees an opportunity to make a statement and it's not about helping the inebriated to enjoy themselves, nor about saving the host from enormous embarrassment.

This statement is about him. Jesus sees the occasion as an opportunity to announce to the world at large that technicolour has arrived. Black and white are no more. We will see in future articles how Jesus brought technicolour into the lives of those he came into contact with, both then and now. But getting back to the wedding, imagine you are the despairing host. A servant brings you a goblet of wine that Jesus produced out of water. Cautiously you taste it. To your utter astonishment, the quality is superior to anything that you spent a fortune on providing yourself. You are overjoyed. Disgrace has been averted. Your reputation is enhanced. You are on cloud nine. Technicolour has arrived, for you and your guests.

In 2010, a bottle of Chateau Lafite-Rothschild 1869 sold for £155,000. That's about £1,350 a sip. Would you like to bet that Jesus' wine was on a par with that? No, Jesus doesn't do black and white.

JESUS DOESN'T DO BLACK AND WHITE (2)

Eusebius, who wrote his history of the Christian Church in the 4th century, told us there was a statue in Edessa, a city now part of Turkey, to a woman who was miraculously healed by Jesus. She had suffered from bleeding for over 12 years but as soon as she touched Jesus' robe the bleeding stopped and she was healed.

For twelve years this woman had been suffering. She had exhausted her wealth on what appears to have been a plethora of doctors, none of whom had helped her but all of whom had taken their fees. Now, she has heard of someone called Jesus who was apparently performing miracles of healing – and he was coming her way. Unfortunately, it seems that everyone else had also heard what Jesus was doing. As a result large crowds were following him wherever he went. However, this woman was desperate. She forced her way through the crowd and just managed to touch Jesus' robe – and was instantly healed.

In Capernaum lay a paralytic. He couldn't use his legs. His friends had also heard of the miracles Jesus was performing. Perhaps Jesus could heal their friend. The only problem? So many people were crowding round that they couldn't reach Jesus in the ordinary way. So they cut a hole in the roof of the house where Jesus was and lowered their friend to the floor. Jesus not only healed him but forgave him his sins as well.

Can you imagine what life must have been like for those two before they met Jesus? Pretty challenging, I would say. Can you imagine what life must have been like for those two after they met Jesus? Well let's give it a try. You have just been told you are through to the final of a major competition. Excited? No? How about finding a hoard of Roman coins on your land worth a fortune? Getting closer? Winning £3million on the lottery? You get the picture? It's in technicolour, isn't it? Jesus doesn't do black and white.

Here are just a couple of extracts from the Bible: *"Jesus went throughout Galilee....healing every disease and sickness.."* *"People brought to him all who were ill with various diseases...and he healed them."* Wherever Jesus travelled he brought relief, freedom from pain, healing from paralysis and much more. Imagine a map of Israel. Stick a pin in it for every place where Jesus healed someone. Now replace each pin with an assortment of coloured paints. See what I mean?

JESUS DOESN'T DO BLACK AND WHITE (3)

"When the sun was setting the people brought to Jesus all who had various kinds of sickness, and laying his hands on each one he healed them"

Once Jesus had been round Israel healing people in body, mind and spirit it must have had a pretty healthy population, compared to other countries. Is it possible, do you think, that we still see in our present age some of the effects of Jesus' ministry? Israel makes up a miniscule 0.2% of the world's population. So how come at least 185 Jews have been awarded a Nobel Prize, accounting for 22% of all individual recipients of the prize worldwide between 1901 and 2011. For example: Jews account for an astonishing 41% of all prize winners in Economics and 27% of all prize winners in Physiology and Medicine. Several reasons have been given. None of them involve Jesus – but I wonder.

It would seem that people who have the technicolour of Jesus in their lives, Jewish or not, make a difference to the world they inhabit. Just think of the impact Mother Theresa had in serving the poor of India. And how about William Wilberforce who ruined his health fighting slavery but lived to see it abolished in the United Kingdom. Then there was Billy Graham who preached directly or indirectly to nearly 215 million people and was spiritual adviser to every American President since Dwight Eisenhower. And think of Charles Colson, disgraced hatchetman for President Nixon, serving time in prison for his role in Watergate. He became a follower of Jesus and founded Prison Christian Fellowship. Today, PCF is present in many prisons of the Western world. All of these Christians brought the technicolour of Jesus to many.

So much for doing things on a grand scale, you might ask, but what about ordinary followers of Jesus? What evidence is there to show that becoming a follower of Jesus changes anything? All I can say is that if you have heard a former prostitute, standing in front of a gathering of many hundreds, admit to her degraded life of paid sex and drugs and see how Jesus has impacted her life. When you hear a politician acknowledge a past of climbing over others to get to the top and committing perjury to hide his guilty behaviour, then see how Jesus has impacted his life, you won't need to ask. Instead you might want that impact in your life by becoming a follower of Jesus yourself. Technicolour awaits.

ARE YOU LISTENING?

Matthew 22

Jesus was a really good storyteller. You probably know that Jesus' mission was to enable us to re-establish the relationship with God that the human race had had until Adam and Eve screwed it up. He demonstrated his power to do this through his healing ministry, through signs and wonders like feeding thousands from a few loaves and fishes, like turning water into wine, like walking on water, like calming the storm and, finally, through overcoming death.

On its own this amazing portfolio wouldn't have done the trick. Oh yes, we might have acknowledged what an amazing person Jesus was, as indeed Napoleon did in one of his more rational moments, but we wouldn't have made the connection. Jesus had to apply the mortar to the bricks to bind them into place. That mortar was his teaching and to get his teaching across he often used stories or parables.

Think, for a moment, of the parable of the wedding banquet. We all love a wedding, don't we? I never turn down an invitation if there's the smallest chance that I can be there. I expect weddings were just as much fun in Jesus' day. The whole village used to turn out when a wedding took place and the feasting could last a week! So when Jesus spoke this parable just about everyone knew what he was talking about.

He said: *"The kingdom of heaven is like a king who prepared a wedding banquet for his son. He sent his servants to those who had been invited to tell them to come but they refused to come. Then he sent some more servants "Tell those who have been invited....everything is ready. Come to the wedding banquet." But they paid no attention and went off – one to his field, another to his business. The rest seized his servants...and killed them. The king was enraged. He sent his army and destroyed those murderers and burned their city."* Jesus finished by saying *"Many are invited but few are chosen."*

So this is what I think the parable means: "I, the God of heaven, prepared a wonderful home for everyone to share with me. I invited you to enjoy what I'd prepared. I sent my prophets and even my son to invite you. Sadly, you shut me out, preferring your businesses, your properties, your celebrity worship, your finances, your sport to me. I have withdrawn your invitation. I shall now invite others who still have room for me in their hearts." Are you listening?

CAN FAITH MAKE YOU WELL?

Luke 17:11
Luke 18:35

It certainly could in Jesus' time. By the time Jesus arrived in the area of Jericho his fame had preceded him and a crowd was accompanying him, presumably to see what would happen next. There was a beggar eking out a paltry living near Jericho. He could hear a crowd passing by but, not being able to see, had to ask what was going on. He was told that Jesus was passing by. So he starts calling out in a loud voice *"Jesus, Son of David, have mercy on me!"* The crowd tells him to stop making a racket but Jesus stops and asks him what he wants. The man replies *"Lord I want to see."* Jesus then utters these remarkable words *"Receive your sight; your faith has healed you."*

Now this is extraordinary. Did this man know Jesus before his arrival? It's doubtful. Clearly he must have heard about him and the miracles he had performed. So he must also have thought, when he heard Jesus was passing by, that if Jesus could heal others perhaps he could heal him. Was that faith? Jesus thought so. Of course, we don't know the whole story. The Bible tells us what we need to know, not always what we would like to know. But it's not the only time that faith made someone well.

On one of his journeys Jesus met ten lepers. They distanced themselves from Jesus because leprosy was thought to be highly infectious in those days. However, they called out in a loud voice *"Jesus, Master, have pity on us!"* Jesus told them to go and show themselves to the priests. On the way there they were healed. One of the ten returns to thank Jesus, falling at his feet. Jesus says to him *"Rise and go; your faith has made you well."*

So much for Jesus' time but what about today? Let's start by asking a sort of reverse question – can depression make you ill? A review of medical opinion on the internet and discussion with a friend who has suffered long makes it clear that depression can come with a variety of symptoms, none of them healthy. According to the internet, the opposite of depression is happiness. I don't think that does the trick. I think contentment with hope for the future is better – being content with who you are, who you love, what you do, what your circumstances are and where you are heading. Being a Christian can give you that. So what's stopping you from becoming one?

"DON'T BE AFRAID; JUST BELIEVE"

Luke 8:40

The Jerusalem leadership had sent us a message warning us to be on our guard against Jesus. The message wasn't clear why. At the synagogue I asked if anyone could enlighten us. Jacob got quite excited. Apparently Jesus was performing all sorts of healing miracles. People were saying he was some sort of prophet, attracting large crowds.

I began to understand the purpose of the message. It appeared some of those who had seen Jesus were asking if he wasn't more than a prophet. There was talk that he might just be the Messiah. Now I could make sense of it. Jesus did not have the stamp of approval from the leadership and we were being warned to steer clear. We all agreed that we would have nothing to do with him.

It was only a couple of weeks later when Jesus had reached the town next to ours that my wife appeared at the synagogue. She was in a terrible state. Our 12 year old daughter was ill. Not just ill, she'd suffered a collapse. She was in bed, couldn't move or eat or anything. I rushed home. As I entered the house I met the doctor on his way out. He shook his head sadly. I have never been so scared. This was our only child and I loved her more than I can say. She looked like death. I didn't know what to do.

Then I recalled the message about Jesus and how he was healing people. I also recalled the message from Jerusalem. I dismissed it. This was my only child. I would do anything for her. I saddled my donkey and rode the short distance to the next town. I forced my way through the large crowd and fell at Jesus' feet, begging him as earnestly and desperately as I could, to come and heal my daughter. To my relief he came.

On our way we met some of my men. My daughter had just died. I was distraught but Jesus said "Don't be afraid; just believe." When we arrived we went into the room where our daughter was lying. Jesus took her by the hand and told her to get up. To our astonishment that's exactly what she did. Then she sat down and ate a meal.

I'm not the synagogue ruler any more but I don't care. As far as I'm concerned, Jesus is the Messiah. And what I say to you is "Don't be afraid; just believe." Who am I? Jairus.

CAN YOU SEE THE PARABLE?

Luke 15:11

Now then Jacob, come and sit at this table in the sun. Then we can watch the world go by, have a chat and enjoy the warmth.

You know, you've had an amazing time of it. Thanks to our friendship I know all about it. You were one of the wealthiest farmers in our village. Then there was that extraordinary situation with your son. I mean, what on earth made you sell up half your land, which is where your wealth came from, and give the proceeds to your younger son? You and your elder son were forced to make all sorts of economies whereas he'd only just come of age and was really not mature enough to handle such wealth.

Sure enough, off he went to the bright lights. All he could think about was himself. We all heard about it. It was absolutely disgraceful. First of all he rented an apartment in the red light area. Then he started throwing his weight and money around like there was no tomorrow. We all knew it couldn't last, even you. It ended in a mess. All his so-called friends deserted him. He had no-one to turn to, got kicked out of the apartment and ended up homeless. Then he got a job looking after pigs. I ask you, how low can anyone go? Then we had a report he was apparently reduced to eating the pig food. He'd really hit rock bottom.

Thank goodness he finally came to his senses and returned home. That certainly vindicated your never giving up hope that he would. To be honest, we used to laugh a bit at the way you would go out looking for him every morning without success - until you were proved right. Then we felt rather bad about our attitude. I can't tell you how touched we were when you actually ran, at your age, to greet him. In our view we thought you had gone way over the top in spoiling him with fine clothes and a party to boot.

My word, how wrong we were. He really was sorry for the way he'd treated you, wasn't he? He said he'd make it up and by golly he did. We've never seen anyone work so hard. Finally, last year he'd earned enough from all his hard work to buy back the half farm that you had to sell.

Quite a story, isn't it? Do you see a parable of God and you in all of this?

SO WHAT DOES THE PARABLE MEAN, THEN?

Luke 15:11

God is our father. He loves us as only a father can. He would give his life for us and, in his son Jesus, that's exactly what he did.

Being a father means that you have to decide how much control to exercise. It's ok when we're very young for our father to be a loving disciplinarian to help us to develop. But as we get older, he encourages us to take responsibility for our own actions. He gives us free will to do as we wish, going our own way. That means we can lose sight of God and become consumed with our own ambitions, desires and challenges - and he lets us. If we didn't have free will we would simply be robots. Now who wants a loving relationship with a robot?

So, off we go, following our own paths. Some of us become very successful and wealthy. Some of us find life a struggle. Some of us haven't got a clue what we should be doing and just drift through life. But there comes a time in all our lives when we will be called to account. We made a lot of money. Did we use it solely for our own benefit? We were down and out. Did we steal from others to keep ourselves going? Some of us looked for a kick out of life. Did we take to drugs and steal from our parents and shops to fund our appetite? Some of us worked really hard. Did we look down on those who didn't? Some of us found being pregnant an inconvenience. Did we have an abortion? Some of us used to abuse our wives. Did we ever consider how they might feel? It will all come out. The question is "When?"

The answer is the sooner the better. Realising that we have made a hash of things and, in so doing, affected the lives of others leaves us with the opportunity to turn back to God. Yes, he is waiting and looking out for us. What's more, he will welcome us with open arms. But we have to come to him in true repentance for all we've done wrong and confess that to him. Then we have the chance to make things right with those we've hurt.

It's a pretty strong parable. In telling it, Jesus was trying to help each one of us see that a future with God is the best way to go. Don't blow it.

DO SOMETHING!

It's interesting to see the circumstances under which Jesus showed his compassion. He wept for Jerusalem because he knew what was going to happen to the city. *"As he approached the city, he wept over it and said, "If you...had only known on this day what would bring you peace – but now it is hidden from your eyes."* He wept for Mary and the sorrowing Jews who had accompanied her to the tomb of her brother, Lazarus. Although he was God he was also a man and showed the emotions of a man. Jesus' weeping was an extension of his compassion.

Think of the two blind men outside Jericho. They knew about Jesus. They heard he was coming their way. So they shouted out, "Lord, Son of David, have mercy on us!" The crowd surrounding Jesus didn't like that one bit. "Leave him alone!" "Stop making that racket!" But that wasn't Jesus' reaction. He had compassion for them. *"What do you want me to do for you?"* He asked and they were healed.

Think of the Greek woman born in Syria. She had a daughter possessed by an evil spirit. She came and fell at Jesus' feet and begged him to heal her daughter. Jesus pointed out to her that his mission was to the Jews *"First let the children eat all they want, for it is not right to take their bread and toss it to the dogs."* What would you have said at that point? Here you are with a sick child. You are desperate. Would you have had the wit and determination to say what the Greek woman said? I'm not sure I would. *"Yes, Lord but even the dogs under the table eat the children's crumbs."* And Jesus replied, *"For such a reply you may go; the demon has left your child."* Jesus' compassion triumphed over mission.

Then there was the woman who had suffered from bleeding for twelve years. She'd tried all the doctors, without success. Perhaps Jesus could do what they couldn't. She reached out and touched his robe. Many people were crowding round Jesus. Yet he knew that power had gone out of him. To him that was the most important thing that had happened then. So he stopped and had compassion on her. The bleeding stopped immediately.

Wherever you look in the four Gospels you see the compassion of Jesus writ large. Would you like that compassion to touch you? Invite Jesus into your life now. Don't wait until you're desperate. A life of thankfulness awaits.

THINGS HAVE CHANGED

Luke 7

I am a prostitute. Or, to put it another way, I was a prostitute – until last week. How did I get into the "profession"? It was my friend Rachel who persuaded me. I made a fair amount of money, of which I put quite a lot into some really expensive perfume. Well, Rachel told me it would be a good investment.

But you know what? I had this awful empty feeling inside me. It wasn't that the neighbours didn't like what I was doing. After all, prostitution had been around for centuries. We had even had temple prostitutes – male and female – in times past. No, this was something that just welled up inside me. I knew it was something to do with the prostitution but what else could I do? The only alternative was to go and work with my cousin Judith in her shawl weaving business. I mean, how dull was that? And it didn't pay very well either. However, I was just getting more and more miserable, hating what I was becoming. Like a disease, this empty feeling hit me every morning as soon as I woke up.

Then I heard about this man, Jesus. People were starting to wonder if he was the Messiah. Judith had been to hear him preach. She told me how he healed people of bad spirits. Privately I wondered if he could do that for me. You see how desperate I was becoming? My chance came fairly soon afterwards. Jesus was dining with a local Pharisee. Alright, yes, he was one of my clients, so I knew I could get into his house without too much effort.

I picked up the only thing of value I had, which was this alabaster jar of perfume, and made my way over to the house. There were quite a few people there but I could immediately tell which one was Jesus. He was reclining at the table with his back to me and his legs outstretched. I just knew he was somebody special. So I went over to him. As I did I just burst into tears and couldn't stop. They fell onto his feet so I wiped them off and then anointed his feet with the perfume, still crying my heart out.

Do you know what he said to me? *"Your sins are forgiven…Your faith has saved you; go in peace"* At that moment my sense of emptiness evaporated. Now I'm working for Judith and I'm happy. Are you?

PRAISE THE LORD. I CAN SEE!

John 9:1

I was blind since birth. Had I missed my sight? Yes, I suppose I had but blindness sort of grew with me. I accepted it as a part of my life. So it's no good asking if I missed it.

Anyway, I was somewhat put out when these men came up and started debating whose fault it was that I couldn't see. What did it matter? It happened. I was blind and that was that. Then their leader said something strange. He said *"...this happened so that the work of God might be displayed in his life."* Well, as you can imagine, that didn't impress me one bit. Not being able to see is not a very good example of the work of God, is it? However, that wasn't what this chap had in mind because he went on *"While I am in the world, I am the light of the world."* I didn't understand that. Would you? But, I tell you what, I did understand it about, I don't know, twenty minutes later.

The next thing that happened is that I hear him scraping some mud off the ground and spitting in it. Then he sticks it on my eyes! Well, thank you! That achieved nothing. I'm just about to wipe it off when he tells me to go to the pool of Siloam and wash there. So I feel my way to the pool, get someone to hold me whilst I lean over the edge and wash my face. Whilst I'm washing I can suddenly see my hands! Then I can see the water! Then I look up and I can see the sky! I can see! I can see everything! I'm not blind anymore!

In my total astonishment and joy I rushed home, quite forgetting to go back and thank whoever it was who healed me. My parents were totally stunned. So was everyone else. They all had to be reassured that I was really who I said I was. Then the Pharisees got in on the act. They just had to investigate and, you know what? The only thing they could come up with was the fact that, according to their ridiculous interpretation of the laws, putting mud on my eyes and healing me was a breach of the Sabbath regulations! Needless to say, I didn't agree with them, got slung out of the synagogue, found Jesus, who had healed me, and put my trust in him. Praise the Lord!

36 HOURS IN THE LIFE OF..... JESUS

- Hear about the death of John the Baptist. John beheaded so Herod could show appreciation for Herodias' daughter's dancing.
- Withdraw by boat to solitary place. Pray to Father. Commend John to him.
- See crowds coming round the side of lake. Well over six or seven thousand, including women and children. Took an hour or so to arrive.
- Have compassion and heal sick of whom there are a large number.
- As it's now getting late, have discussion with disciples about how to feed the crowd. Disciples want them to go but opportunity to bring glory to Father.
- We produce five loaves and two fishes. Look up to heaven and give thanks to Father. Break up loaves. Then give to disciples to give to the people. There's enough to go round. Not only does everyone

get fed and is satisfied but there are twelve baskets of broken pieces of bread left over. When will they understand?

– Send disciples off in boat to sail to the other side of the lake.

– Once everyone departed go up mountainside to pray. Spend most of night in touch with Father.

– Sometime between 3.00 and 6.00am decide to catch up with disciples. Now they are in middle of lake and making heavy weather of it as wind is against them. Quickest way to get there is to walk out to the boat, across the lake.

– When they see me they think it's a ghost so have to reassure them. Then Peter, always the brash one, says if it's me tell him to come out to me. He gets out of the boat and walks halfway to me but then gets scared of the waves. Have to rescue him. Say "O you of little faith. Why did you doubt." Hope this is a lesson that will resound down through the ages.

– Can hear disciples marvelling and recognising me as Son of God. Will it last?

– Reach Gennesaret and land. People flock from countryside, bringing their sick. Can see I'm tired. They ask if they can just touch the edge of my cloak. All who do are healed.

– Another run-in with the Pharisees and teachers of the law. This time they're complaining about disciples not washing their hands before eating. Use the occasion to give some teaching about what is really clean and unclean. Pharisees – hypocrites!

Was ever a country as blessed as Israel to have Jesus live there?

A TALE OF TWO CITIES

John 8:3

My name is Aalilyah. I won't give you my family name as I don't want to bring any more shame on them. I used to live in Tehran. Where I live now doesn't really matter. So why am I kneeling down in front of a grave with my arms bound behind my back? It's because I have been found guilty of adultery and am about to be shot. It's true, I am – guilty - that is. I loved my husband but I fell. It was my boss. He kept on flattering me and giving me admiring glances. I could cope with that but then he started leaving packets of money under my blotting pad. I was able to buy all sorts of things for myself I had not been able to afford. I had to leave them at the office but, I admit, I wanted more. On one occasion he left an invitation to what I thought was a talk by a woman I have a great admiration for. She fights for women's rights. So I accepted. It turned out it was a hoax. He actually took me to his house. His wife was away and there were no staff there. So we frolicked in the swimming pool and, you can imagine the rest. At which point his wife returned unexpectedly....so here I am, about to die.

My name is Batsheva. I live in Jerusalem. I'm named after King David's wife. You know, the one who took a bath in full view of David and roused him lust. I guess I'm not badly named, because that's sort of what I did. Well, I was bored. My parents had married me to an oaf just because they wanted the dowry which was a field next to theirs. So when this young couple moved in next door, I couldn't help noticing how handsome the husband was. I'm not bad looking either, even though I say so myself. Anyway, one thing led to another and before you knew it, we were in bed together. That's when her mother came over to change the straw mattresses and found us there. So I was brought in front of man named Jesus by the Pharisees. They wanted to stone me in accordance with the Mosaic law but he said "Let him who is without sin cast the first stone" and they all disappeared, leaving me standing there. "Go and sin no more", he said. So I did and I'm not going to mess up again, that's for sure.

WELL, WHY DID YOU INVITE HIM?

Luke 14

Wife: "Well, why did you invite him? I'm pretty sure he was still in his working clothes. And did you notice that he didn't wash his hands? Then he cured the foot-washing slave of his dropsy – and on a Sabbath to boot. No wonder everyone was wondering what on earth he was doing at one of our key dinners. I mean, aren't we out to impress the hierarchy? You know, the members of the Sanhedrin and the teachers of the law? We spent hours going over the guest list, where they'd sit, what they'd eat. Also, we spent a fortune sorting out the food. Then you had to go and invite this nonentity to join us at the last minute. Have you any idea how much upset you caused by inviting him to sit next to you? At least three members of the Sanhedrin had their noses put out of joint by having to move further down the table. Sometimes it seems to me you just don't think before you act."

Husband: "Actually, this is what I was thinking. The annual meeting of the Sanhedrin is coming up soon. That's when they decide who gets promoted into more senior positions. Well, I've got my eye on becoming Treasurer. There's even more money to be made in that job than just about any other, apart from the position of Chief Priest, which I've also got my eye on, but not for the immediate future. Now this fellow, Jesus, has been upsetting the Council. For a start, every member they've sent to try to catch him out has made a complete mess of it. He's had an answer to everything they've thrown at him so far.

So, at our weekly meeting yesterday the Chief Priest issued a general invitation for any of us who reckoned we could get the better of Jesus to give it a go. He even went so far as to hint that "rewards " would await the person who could demonstrate that Jesus was a fraud. Now, I reckon I'm smarter than most of the other members so, when I heard Jesus was in the locality it made sense to invite him along. Just think what an impression I would have made in front of my fellow guests if I had shown him up."

Wife: "Well, you certainly made a mess of that. Talk about embarrassment!"
Husband: "I know, I'll just have to think of some other way to make money."

WELCOME TO MY HUMBLE ABODE

John 11

Hello everyone! Welcome to my humble abode. You can't all get inside but I hope you can hear me anyway. We've lived here for 35 years as a lot of people can testify. That's me and my two sisters, Mary and Martha. We're giving this dinner in honour of Jesus. He's sitting on my right. You may not know him but, by the time I've finished you'll wish you did because what I'm about to tell you is absolutely true. Feel free to ask around afterwards.

Six weeks ago I went down with a fever. Usually these things pass after a while, but not this one. It got worse and worse. I could see from my sisters' faces that they feared the worst. And that's what happened. I weakened until I couldn't take any medicines or food and, basically, just gave up the ghost and died. It's true. Look, why don't you check this out for a couple of minutes? There are plenty here who saw what happened.....

Now at this point I obviously didn't have a clue what happened next, so I'm going to hand over to Mary whilst Martha gets on with serving the dinner." 'Evening everyone. Yes, I'm Mary. Well, as you can imagine, we were distraught. Who was going to look after the fields? How would we manage? But first, we had to bury Lazarus. So we wrapped him up and anointed him in the usual manner and arranged for Isaac the carrier to transport his body to our family tomb, which was more of a cave than anything else. We put him in there and laid a large stone across the entrance. Then we went home and started sorting out Lazarus' things, getting ready to sell off what we could. That took us about three days.

On the fourth day, Jesus arrived and Martha went out to meet him, explaining everything. Then I did and together we went to the tomb. I really didn't know what was going to happen but Jesus obviously did because he told the crowd to take the stone away. Then he looked up to heaven and said in a loud voice "Lazarus, come out!" I'd better hand over to Lazarus at this point."

"Thanks, Mary. I can't explain it. All I know is that suddenly I was awake. I was able to walk but I needed help to get all the grave-clothes off. To conclude I can tell you that Jesus is the source of life. I am the living proof."

DAD, YOU KEEP GOING ON ABOUT PROPHECIES

Dad: "Well, son, just think about it for a minute. If I told you that you would win the 400 metres race at your school sports and you did, what would you think?"
Son: "Not a lot, because you know I won the race last year."
Dad: Precisely, but suppose I told you that you would marry Elaine Thompson, have three children, end up as Managing Director of BT and retire to a nice house in Somerset. You'd think I was mad, until it happened, wouldn't you?"
Son: "Well, I would be totally astonished that you had such extraordinary powers of prophecy. I would ask myself if I hadn't underestimated you."
Dad: "The people who wrote the Old Testament were in the same position. They prophesied that certain things about the Messiah, that's Jesus, would happen, and they did. They're all recorded in the Bible. Perhaps you need to ask yourself if you haven't underestimated those who wrote the Bible."

Son: "Before I do, can you give me some examples?"

Dad: "There are over 300 prophecies which have been fulfilled, some fairly general, others very precise but I'll only look at a few:

<u>Birthplace:</u> "But as for you, Bethlehem Ephrathah..From you one will go forth...to be ruler in Israel." Micah 5:2. Jesus was born in Bethlehem.

<u>Miracles:</u> "Then the eyes of the blind will be opened... the ears of the deaf unstopped...the lame will leap like a deer and the tongue of the dumb will shout for joy". Isaiah 35:5. Jesus went about healing every kind of disease and sickness.

<u>Entry into Jerusalem:</u> "Behold your king is coming to you, mounted on a donkey, even on a colt, the foal of a donkey." Zechariah 9:9. Jesus entered Jerusalem, prior to his death, on a colt, the foal of a donkey.

<u>Betrayal:</u> "Even my close friend... has lifted up his heel against me." Psalm 41:9. Jesus was betrayed by Judas Iscariot, one of his disciples.

<u>False witnesses:</u> " Malicious witnesses rise up." Psalm 35:11. The chief priest brought forward false witnesses to accuse Jesus.

<u>Crucifixion:</u> "They pierced my hands and my feet" Psalm 22:16. Jesus' crucifixion involved the nailing of hands and feet.

None of these prophecies was dated closer to the events they covered than about 500 years. If you want a fuller picture, I can refer you to Josh McDowell's "Evidence that demands a verdict" that covers many more of the prophecies. Interested?"

Son: "No thanks, Dad. I'm convinced.

Dad: "Let's hope the readers are as well."

SYMMETRY – DONKEYS

At the end of his ministry Jesus gave Peter his mission when he returned from fishing. I think there's also a symmetry about donkeys.

Whilst Mary was expecting Jesus and was engaged to Joseph, Caesar Augustus issued a decree that a census should be taken of the entire Roman world, which included Israel. This required everyone to return to the town of their lineage. In Joseph's case this was Bethlehem because he was of David's lineage and Bethlehem was the town of David. Now, it's a journey of 70 miles from Nazareth to Bethlehem. Is it reasonable to suppose that a pregnant woman would be able to walk that distance? Not if she was heavily pregnant. The Bible doesn't make clear just how pregnant Mary was but it's reasonable to assume that she was heavily pregnant because she gave birth in Bethlehem. After all, if she was only lightly pregnant wouldn't she have wanted to return to Nazareth where her mother and close family would have been on hand to give support and encouragement?

So, if she was heavily pregnant, she would have found it incredibly difficult to walk 70 miles, particularly over the sort of terrain that exists in Israel. It therefore seems not unreasonable that Joseph would have found a donkey for her to ride – and goodness knows that must have been pretty uncomfortable anyway. It wouldn't have been a horse. Horses were for gentry and the military.

Thus, on the way to the place of his birth, it's reasonable to suppose that Jesus was "riding" a donkey.

On the way to the place of his death Jesus was riding a donkey. He didn't own one. In fact, he walked everywhere during the time of his three- year ministry. So the Bible makes special mention that: "...*at the hill called the Mount of Olives, he sent two of disciples, saying.."Go to the village ahead of you, and as you enter it, you will find a colt* (the word used means "donkey") *tied there...untie it and bring it here. If anyone asks you tell him "The Lord needs it."* That's symmetry for you but it gets better.

In the book of Zechariah in the Old Testament we find these words *"See, your king comes to you, righteous and having salvation, gentle and riding on a donkey, on a colt the foal of a donkey."* That's symmetry, right?

HAVE WE GOT ENOUGH EVIDENCE TO KILL HIM?

High Priest: "Alright, Obadiah. What evidence can you put to the Sanhedrin?

Obadiah: "I've been keeping a record for almost two years.

1. He comes from Galilee and you know nothing good comes from there.
2. In his first sermon he tells everyone that they've got to be more righteous than us if they want to get into heaven. What cheek!

3. Then there was another dig at us when he said people (meaning us) shouldn't stand on street corners to be seen when they pray. Don't we need to be seen?

4. He completely broke our rules when he went to eat with tax collectors and sinners. Fine example!

5 He broke our rules when he and his disciples didn't fast. He's mocking us.

6. Then he started talking about his father in heaven. If that isn't blasphemy I don't know what is.

7. He's definitely going to stir up trouble because I heard him say he wasn't bringing peace but a sword. Then he said he was going to destroy family harmony by turning sons against fathers, daughters against mothers and so on. Personally, I think he's mad or demon-possessed.

8. Then, believe it or not, he and his accursed disciples starting picking corn on the Sabbath.

9. Shortly after that he healed a demon-possessed man which, to my mind proves he's demon-possessed.

10. When I and some teachers of the law asked him for a sign, he then likened himself to Jonah and said he'd spend three days and nights in the earth – and presumably come back to life again. What a laugh!

11. Also, disgusting habit, he doesn't wash his hands before meals thereby breaking the tradition of the elders. Talk about throwing his weight around.

12. Then he had the cheek to advise his followers to be on their guard – against us!

13. It gets worse. He comes to the temple and throws out all the contractors we've engaged, saying "My house is a house of prayer but you (meaning us!) are making it a den of thieves"

14. He then tells a parable which concludes with him saying that tax collectors and prostitutes will enter the Kingdom of God ahead of us. Ridiculous!

15. Finally, he launches into a direct tirade against us, calling us hypocrites, blind fools, blind guides and white-washed tombs. He's got to be stopped.

High Priest: "We've heard enough. Temple guards! Find a way to arrest him.
Zachariah: " But High Priest, what if he's right?"

WAS JESUS IN CONTROL?

The Four Gospels

In the short period covering Jesus' arrest, trial before the Sanhedrin, trial before Pontius Pilate and crucifixion – described in some detail in the four gospels – a number of things happened to Jesus that lead one to question whether he was really in control of what was going on.

I know it's difficult, given the two millennia that have passed since that fateful time, but I want you to imagine you are in Jesus' position.

You are praying on the Mount of Olives when Judas, the betrayer, arrives with a group of functionaries and soldiers sent by the Sanhedrin to arrest you. You are taken before Caiaphas, the high priest and the Sanhedrin. They conduct a trial which is a farce and gets them precisely nowhere. Finally you are asked outright if you are *"the Christ, the Son of the Blessed One."* You confirm that you are. This is pure blasphemy in the eyes of the court, deserving of death. What follows is a disgrace.

Members of the Sanhedrin come up to you and spit in your face. So now you have several people's saliva running down your face. You are then blindfolded. The next thing that happens is that someone punches you in the face. You are not able to anticipate this so you stagger backwards trying to keep your balance. Then someone else hits you in the face and you fall over. In addition to the saliva running down your face, you are now bleeding from your nose, one of your eyes hurts and so does your shoulder from where you hit the floor.

At this point you are pulled to your feet by the guards who set about beating you all over. Your ribs are bruised, your stomach hurts and both your ears ache. Are you imagining this? You are not in a very good condition, are you? You are probably thrown into a cell for the short remainder of the night. Early the next morning you are bound, not that you are in any condition to run away, and taken before Pontius Pilate, the Roman Governor, who alone has the power to sentence you to death by crucifixion. Now your already cruel treatment takes a turn for the worse.

Pilate orders you to be flogged and then crucified. When the Jews flogged someone they stopped after 39 lashes. They didn't want to exceed 40 lashes so stopped short by one just in case. Wasn't that considerate? The Romans observed no such restriction. Welcome to hell.

WAS JESUS IN CONTROL? (2)

Remember, you are imagining yourself in Jesus' position. You have been taken before Pontius Pilate and he has ordered you to be flogged. I am afraid you are not going to like this. Let me tell you why.

The instrument used was a flagellum, like a cat o' nine tails. It had at least three strands. These strands were weighted with lead balls or pieces of bone. They were designed to lacerate. Eusebius, a church historian of the fourth century, in his history of the church, described what happened. *"For they say that the bystanders were struck with amazement when they saw them lacerated with scourges, even to the innermost veins and arteries, so that the hidden inward parts of the body, both their bowels and their members, were exposed to view."*

The victim of a flogging was left in unimaginable pain and near the point of death. When allied to a crucifixion, the flogging would be severe. Why? Because the Roman soldiers had to guard the crosses until the victims had died. Clearly they didn't want to be hanging around all night, (if you'll pardon the pun) so a severe flogging would hasten the victim's end.

So, you have now been flogged. Your pain is indescribable. You are near the point of death. I won't ask you how you're feeling but I am sorry to tell you that your tribulations are not over yet. The Roman soldiers come together and put a purple robe on you, then twist together a crown of thorns and no doubt some of the thorns will have pricked your scalp in a rather painful way. Did you notice that above the pain you are already suffering? Even if you didn't you will notice what happens next because you are going to be hit on the head with a staff, not once or twice but again and again. Oh yes, one final insult before taking you off to be crucified, they spit on you. That's the second time that's happened.

Now you are going to be crucified. Ordinarily, the victim would be forced to carry his own cross. Sadly, you are in no condition to do that. You probably don't have a back to carry the cross on. So Simon who comes from Cyrene, a Roman city in what is now Cyrenaica, Libya, has to carry the cross for you, whilst you stagger up the hill leaking blood all the way. I wonder if you're even going to notice when they nail you to the cross.

WAS JESUS IN CONTROL? (3)

Jesus has been nailed to a cross. The experience has been awful. Was Jesus in control?

There are two factors about Jesus' life that are relevant. The first is that he always did the will of his Father. *"For I have come down from heaven....to do the will of him who sent me."* We see this in the time of prayer, shortly before Jesus' arrest. Jesus knew what he was in for. Listen to him pray in anguish: *"Father, if you are willing, take this cup from me; yet not my will but yours be done.* Left alone, Jesus might just have weakened and avoided the agony. It was his Father's will that he should die and he obeyed.

The second point is Jesus' fulfillment of prophecy. *"I did not come to abolish the Law or the Prophets (prophecy)…. but to fulfill them."* There are about 300 prophecies in the Old Testament which relate to the Messiah. 29 of those related to the period from Jesus' arrest to his death on the cross and burial. All of them were fulfilled.

Jesus went to the cross in obedience to his Father and in fulfillment of Prophecy. But there's more. Can you recall the state you were in when you were imagining being nailed to the cross? What would you have been saying there, if anything? Groaning? Crying out in agony? Cursing those who put you there? Praying for a quick death? We know what Jesus said. It's none of the above. First he takes care of one of the criminals crucified with him: *"Today you will be with me in Paradise."* Then he takes care of those who crucified him: *"Father, forgive them for they do not know what they are doing."* Then he takes care of his mother: *"Dear Woman, here is your son."* (Probably meaning John) and to John: *"Here is your mother."*

Only after that is he concerned for himself. That is when all the sins of the world descend on him. All the child abuses, rapes, wife-beatings, immorality, murders, tortures, burglaries, thefts, arsons, adulteries, cruelties, drunken behaviour, drug abuse, kidnappings, greed, selfishness and thousands of other sins separate him from a holy God: *"My God, my God, why have you forsaken me?"*

Jesus' last words were *"It is finished,"* his mission on earth accomplished. Do you think it's possible Jesus was in control? And can you imagine how much God loves you to ask his own and only son to experience such an agonising death – for you? Makes you think?

SATAN'S CUNNING PLANS

Right, gather round! We've got a situation here. I thought I'd messed up God's plan for Israel. Introducing women who brought their own gods with them, married Israelites and got them to worship their gods was a brilliant idea. God sent Israel into exile. When they came back they were a pitiful bunch.

However, to my astonishment God didn't give up on them. Now he's planning to send his son to rescue not only the Israelites but all of mankind. It's just not on. Something has to be done about it. Any ideas? What's that? Divert Jesus before he can fulfil his mission? What? Like I did with Adam and Eve? That worked really well. So what I need to do is separate him from his Father and I know how to do that. OK. I'll do it.......

.......It didn't work! I tried putting doubt into his mind like I did with Eve. "If you are the son of God..." I did it twice and quoted the bible to support my suggestions but each time he quoted some other biblical line to rebut me. Finally I got fed up with wheedling and tried to bribe him with everything I could throw into the pot. I showed him all the kingdoms of the world and their splendour and said "All this I will give you if you will bow down and worship me." If he'd fallen for it I would have beaten God because what else could he do after losing his son but destroy the world again. But he didn't fall for it.

So here we are facing a crisis. But I know what I am going to do. I am not going to take him on by the direct approach. I am going to get those idiot earthlings that he loves so much to do it for me. Here's how it's going to work. He might demonstrate all sorts of miracles, signs and wonders but it won't cut the mustard with the people in authority. I will encourage them to see him as a disruption to their tidy, little lives. An offence in their nostrils. I will get them to kill him. If I do it myself God will deal with me in a most unpleasant way and I don't want that.

Not only will they kill him by crucifixion but they will mock and scorn him and have him beaten almost to death before he even gets to that. Wonderful. Nothing good can happen after he's dead..........can it?

IT'S NEVER TOO LATE

2 Chronicles 29 & 30
Luke 23:40

Hezekiah was twenty-five years old when he became King of Judah. The Bible tells us that he did what was right in the eyes of the Lord. He calls together all those involved in running the temple and this is what he says:

"Our fathers were unfaithful; they did evil in the eyes of the Lord our God and forsook him....Therefore the anger of the Lord has fallen on Judah and Jerusalem;

he has made them an object of dread and horror and scorn, as you can see with your own eyes. This is why our fathers have fallen by the sword and why our sons and daughters and wives are in captivity. Now I intend to make a covenant with the Lord, the God of Israel, so that his fierce anger will turn away from us."

Hezekiah was the 33rd of the 40 kings of Israel and Judah. When he talks of his fathers, he was referring to the bulk of those who ruled before him. They had dishonoured and disobeyed God. No wonder God's "fierce anger" had fallen on the Israelites. However, Hezekiah knew that if Israel repented and turned back to God he would turn his anger away, even after all the evil they had done. So he had the temple cleansed and made sacrifices to remove Israel's guilt.

There is a telling comment that follows the description of the cleansing and sacrifices that took place. It states *"and the Lord heard Hezekiah and healed the people."* It's never too late.

Two criminals were crucified at the same time as Jesus. We don't know what it was they had done to deserve such a ghastly death but it must have been really bad. Listen to what one of them says to the other from his cross, as Jesus was nailed to his:

"Don't you fear God, since you are under the same sentence? We are punished justly, for we are getting what our deeds deserve. But this man has done nothing wrong. Jesus, remember me when you come into your kingdom."

In other words, even as he was dying this criminal recognised that he had done wrong, was undoubtedly sorry for that, recognised that Jesus was who he said he was and was putting his trust in Jesus to rectify the situation. And Jesus responded. Here's what he said: "… *today you will be with me in paradise."*

Now there's a message. It's never too late to repent and put your trust in Jesus. Why don't you?

LIFE WILL NEVER BE THE SAME

Matthew 27 & 28

We were there. The disciples had all fled when Jesus was arrested, except for Peter and he'd disowned Jesus. Jesus had to take the path to crucifixion on his own. We women didn't dare get close but stood at a distance, watching. I can't tell you how awful it was. It broke our hearts, not only to see Jesus suffer and die in agony but also to see such a degrading end to the wonderful ministry we had witnessed over the last few years - his kindness and compassion for the sick and poor, the way he healed them and taught those who were prepared to listen. And now it was all over. We would be returning to our homes in Galilee with nothing to look forward to. I can't tell you how miserable we were. There was just one thing left to do, say goodbye.

We watched as Joseph came forward, one follower at least of Jesus who hadn't fled. He took Jesus' body, wrapped it in a cloth and placed it in his own new tomb. He then rolled in a large stone to block the entrance and went away. We'd followed him to the tomb, so knew where Jesus was. Then we went off to our dwelling because the next day was the Sabbath. We spent it in abject misery.

The next day, everything changed. After breaking our fast, we went back to the tomb again, to be near Jesus. Have you ever seen an angel? Just as we arrived at the tomb one came down from heaven in the middle of an earthquake that was so violent it threw us off our feet. His appearance was like lightning and his clothes were white as snow. The tomb guards promptly fainted. I felt like fainting as well.

"Don't be afraid," he said, *"for I know you are looking for Jesus, who was crucified. He is not here. He has risen, just as he said. Come and see where he lay. Then go quickly and tell his disciples."* We hurried away, afraid yet filled with joy and, suddenly, it happened. There was Jesus, alive! We fell at his feet. *"Do not be afraid,"* he said, *"Go and tell my brothers to go to Galilee; there they will see me."*

Why did he show himself first to us? Could it be because we stayed with him to the end or, should I say, beginning? No, life will never be the same.

DID JESUS RISE FROM THE DEAD?

(1 Corinthians Chapter 5 Verses 1-8)

St Paul put it very well in one of his first century letters *"If Christ has not been raised your faith is futile."*

However, he adds *"But Christ has indeed been raised from the dead…"* How did he know? How could he be so definite?

Paul could have known first, from personal experience. He encountered Jesus on the road to Damascus. It's a gripping story, recorded in chapter 9 of the Book of Acts in the New Testament. Well worth a read. After that encounter Paul was a changed man. Secondly, he listened to the experiences of others. We know Paul spent time with Jesus' disciples. They must have compared notes. The disciples were not laggard in speaking out about their faith in Jesus, even under intense pressure.

We have records of the prosecution of disciples dating back to the early years. From them we could compile an imaginary court case:

<u>Procurator</u> "Now then, tell me about your time with Jesus before he was crucified."

<u>Phillip</u> "Well, we hung out with him and he did all sorts of amazing stuff that no-one else could do. We really thought he was sent by God to become King of Israel and throw out the Romans."

<u>Procurator</u> "So the fact that he was crucified must have dealt a devastating blow to your expectations?"

<u>Phillip</u> "Too right! The moment he got himself arrested we all scarpered.

<u>Procurator</u> So why were you arrested outside the temple for preaching that Jesus was the Son of God and had risen from the dead?"

<u>Phillip</u> "'cause that's what he did! He came back. We saw him. We touched him. We ate with him. We

saw his wounds. He's alive I tell you. I'll never worship anyone else. Jesus is the Son of God. And you'd better listen to me because, if you put your trust in him and become a follower you will be forgiven your sins and find eternal life. Otherwise, you're damned to hell."

<u>Procurator</u> "Now we're getting to the crux of the matter. Swear allegiance to the Emperor or follow your Son of God to the cross. What do you say?"

<u>Phillip</u> "Do what you like to me – and be damned. I have only one ruler and that's Jesus, my King."

Now readers might say "You're just asking us to rely on what's in the Bible. How do we know the Bible isn't a myth or been changed over the centuries? Well, we'll look at that in a future edition of the Magazine.

WELL, WHAT WOULD YOU HAVE SAID?

John 20:24

You've had a lousy day at the office. Nothing has gone right. You're boss has had you in twice to discuss issues that have raised all sorts of difficulties. He's giving out negative vibes. As you make your way home from the station you're not looking forward to getting home and having to deal with your wife's complaints about the children misbehaving. Unusually, your wife is waiting for you on the doorstep. She can hardly speak she is so excited. "We've won the lottery. It's more than five million."

Jesus liked Thomas. He must have done because he chose him to be one of his disciples. And Thomas must have liked Jesus because he stuck with him right

139

to the end. It was just his bad luck not to be present when Jesus first appeared to his disciples after his resurrection. So, imagine this scenario. You are Thomas. You are out and about on some sort of mission, probably finding provisions but doing it in the dark and pulling your cloak over your head so the authorities won't recognise you.

You return to the accommodation and find the disciples in an uproar. Everybody is shouting at once, hugging each other, praising God and jumping about. It's all about seeing Jesus alive, back from the dead. They're rubbing their eyes and saying things like "It's true." "Didn't he say he would?" "What's he's going to do next?" You can hardly make sense of it. Half of you thinks they're all drunk. Gradually, silence falls. They're all waiting for you to say something. Well, do you want to stop and have a think about what to say? I might have said "Well, where is he then?" But might you have said what Thomas said?

"Unless I see the nail marks in his hands and put my fingers where the nails were and put my hand into his side I will not believe it." If so, then as the "Dad" mentioned above you might have said "That's wonderful but do you mind if I check the ticket?" Is that what you thought you would have said? Then you might have some sympathy for Thomas? Didn't he say what a sensible, rational person might have said?

Jesus liked Thomas. He showed him his wounds and Thomas believed. Jesus said *"Because you have seen me, you have believed; blessed are those who have not seen and yet have believed."* Now there's a thought.

SYMMETRY – FISH

John 21

There is a lot of symmetry in the Bible. Take fish, for example. We all know that Peter was fishing when Jesus chose him to be a disciple. He wasn't catching anything until Jesus told him to go out and fish again. When he did, he and his partners caught so many fish that their net began to break.

Then, right at the end of John's Gospel, we find Peter fishing again. Let's look at the context. Jesus had been crucified but not before Peter had denied three times that he knew him. Then Jesus rises from the dead. He appears to the disciples. So far so good. But what future role there is for the disciples is not yet clear to us. Nor does it seem clear to them. Why? Because Peter goes fishing. Why does he go fishing? Because that's what he used to do before Jesus came along and made him one of his disciples. In other words, Peter has gone back to his roots, doing what he knew before Jesus came along. It seems to the disciples that the "party" is over.

So what better way for Jesus to demonstrate to Peter and the other disciples that their mission is imminent than to adopt the same way of calling them that he used at the start of his earthly ministry? The first time Jesus met Peter fishing he took him away to spend three years observing, discussing and participating – seeing Jesus work out his mission on earth. The second time? Well let's review the position.

We find Peter and his comrades spending the night fishing – and catching nothing, just like it was the first time. Jesus appears to them and again gives them directions to ensure they catch fish by throwing the net over the other side of the boat. When they do they catch 153 large fish. The haul was so large that they couldn't get the net into the boat but had to haul it ashore. Do you see the symmetry? I'm pretty sure Peter does.

That's where the symmetry ends because Jesus is not going to spend another three years teaching disciples through his ministry. They are going to be the ministers from now on. Look at how Jesus commissions Peter. Three times Jesus asks Peter if he loves him. Three times Peter affirms that he does. Three times Jesus responds: *"Feed my lambs"*, *"Take care of my sheep"*, *"Feed my sheep"*. Peter has been given his ministry. It will take him to the cross.

AN INTERVIEW WITH PETER

Ralph: "Many thanks for coming in, Peter. Can you tell us how you became a Christian?"

Peter: "Good morning, Ralph. Delighted to be here. If I can just correct one point? We didn't call ourselves Christians, at least not to start with. Followers of Jesus was who we were. And, of course, if I can say so without appearing proud, I was also hugely privileged to be one of the twelve disciples. So, to answer your question, I was called by Jesus. As you probably know, I was out fishing when Jesus first appeared. His manner and his air of authority seemed to demand unquestioning obedience. So I gave up my lucrative way of life and followed him.

However, I think there's more to your question than that. It wasn't until Jesus came back to life after his crucifixion that it really dawned on me that I had made a lifelong commitment, whatever the consequences. As you know, up to that point I was ready to give all that up."

R: "That's really what I was coming on to. What were you like before Jesus met up with you after coming back to life?"

P: "The word that comes to mind is "Flakey". I couldn't be relied on. Jesus treated me really well. He told me I would have a position of great authority. He made me one of his closest circle and I let him down time and time again, even denying I knew him whilst he was undergoing his awful trial. I was rash, made promises I couldn't keep. You've no idea how ashamed I was."

R: "So how have you changed?

P: "That's probably for others to say but if there's one word that sums me up now it's "Grateful". Of course I faced trials and torments of my own but I know I came through them with my integrity intact. The reason I was able to do so was the realisation first that Jesus was really who he said he was – the Son of God. Secondly, that he proved this in the most dramatic way, by conquering death. Thirdly, knowing exactly what I was like he forgave me all the shameful nonsenses I had perpetrated. Fourthly, he gave me the most earth-shattering mission, to preach the gospel to all the world."

R: "So what would you say to someone who was thinking of becoming a follower of Jesus?"

P: "Don't delay. Jesus is waiting with outstretched arms to welcome you into his Kingdom."

HAD PETER REALLY CHANGED?

1 Peter

Peter was grateful for everything Jesus had done for him. But had he put that gratitude into practice? It needed to be checked out. The only evidence available is in the Acts of the Apostles and the two letters he wrote that we read in the Bible. This is how the first one starts.

"To God's elect, strangers in the world." He was reminding us that our life on earth is temporary and our real home is in heaven. We are passing through. Travel lightly.

"who have been chosen according to the foreknowledge of God the Father, through the sanctifying work of the Spirit, for obedience to Jesus Christ and sprinkling by his blood." God loves everyone. But he knows who will make a commitment to him and who will reject him. Those who make the right decision will be made holy through the work of the Holy Spirit and the sacrifice of Jesus. Have you made your decision?

"Praise be to the God and Father of our Lord Jesus Christ! In his great mercy he has given us new birth into a living hope through the resurrection of Jesus Christ from the dead, and into an inheritance that can never perish, spoil or fade – kept in heaven for you..." When we make a real and deep commitment to Jesus we acquire a new life. We are born again. Are you born again? Do you rest on the living hope that you have an inheritance that can never perish, spoil or fade?

"Though you have not seen him, you love him; and even though you do not see him now, you believe in him and are filled with an inexpressible and glorious joy, for you are receiving the goal of your faith, the salvation of your souls." This is what Peter himself must have experienced otherwise he couldn't possibly have written these words. He knew he had let Jesus down in a big way and been forgiven. Are you filled with an inexpressible and glorious joy?

"Prepare your minds for action; be self-controlled, set your hope fully on the grace to be given you when Jesus Christ is revealed." How do you convert inexpressible and glorious joy into action? By preparing your minds, being self-controlled and living in anticipation of a wonderful future.

How could the Peter who had made a mess of everything write such words? Either he was a hypocrite of the worst order or he really had been changed through being been born again. Are you? Do you want to be? Call the office.

NO, I DIDN'T UNDERSTAND

Yes, I was one of his disciples. No, I didn't choose him; he chose me. Why, I really can't say.

I hadn't a clue about what I had let myself in for. I just knew that, in some way, we were going to be fishers of men, whatever that meant.

So we started out, walking everywhere. That was alright; we were used to that. But then things started happening. First of all we headed for Galilee. Wherever we went Jesus took us into the local synagogue and started preaching what he called the good news about the Kingdom. That was on the Sabbath. Then he'd preach to large crowds in the open air during the week. I thought that was great. I was all in favour of the Kingdom, whatever that was, because I was bound to have an important position in it if I stuck close to Jesus. But he also used parables as well and I have to say I didn't understand those too well. Nor did the other disciples. We used to get Jesus to explain them to us.

However, things got even better when he started healing people. It was quite amazing really. No-one had ever seen anything like it. People came from all over the place, bringing their sick with them and he healed the lot – those with severe pain, the demon-possessed, those having seizures, the paralysed – all of them. I enjoyed being a part of his group. People were really pleased to see us as well as him. I even managed to heal some people myself.

There were lots of other astonishing things, like walking on water, calming storms, turning water into wine. We knew we'd hitched up with someone special. Just when I began wondering when we were going to head for Jerusalem and take over there things took a turn for the worse, much worse in fact. Jesus started explaining to us that he must go to Jerusalem and suffer many things at the hands of the elders, chief priests and teachers of the law, be killed and on the third day be raised to life. Well, that didn't sound like someone taking over and establishing a Kingdom, nor did I see how I was going to benefit from all of that.

But it was the last part that really got me. I mean, come on! Who on earth gets raised to life after being killed. You'd have to be God for that to happen. So no, I didn't understand..... I do now.

SYMMETRY – CLOTHES

Exodus 39: 22,23
John 19:23

Son: "Dad, you keep going on about symmetry but, to be honest, some of your examples are a bit wishy-washy. Have you got any others?"

Dad: "Ignoring your unjustified criticism, which I will leave for another time, I have one that's been exercising me lately."

S: "Oh? What's that?"

D: "You know I'm working my way through Exodus at the moment? Some of it's a bit hard going but if you persevere there are lots of gems to be discovered. Let me show you one. If you turn to Exodus 39 you will find there a description of the priestly garments. You know, the ephod, the breastpiece and so on. What's interesting, though, is that you get a detailed description of how the robe of the ephod was made. *"They made the robe of the ephod entirely of blue cloth – the work of a weaver – with an opening in the centre of the robe like the opening of a collar, and a band around this opening, so that it would not tear."* In other words, it seems to me that it was a seamless robe. Now where have I come across that before?"

S: "I know, Dad. Didn't Jesus have one?"

D: "That's right! The soldiers who were guarding the crucifixion site had the dubious privilege of sharing out the clothes of the crucifixion victims. This is what John tells us: *"When the soldiers crucified Jesus, they took his clothes, dividing them into four shares, one for each of them, with the undergarment remaining. This garment was seamless, woven in one piece from top to bottom"*. Now the question is, "Why on earth should Jesus' undergarment warrant a mention? I mean here's the Son of God dying for us and the disciple thinks the fact that the soldiers cast lots for his undergarment is noteworthy."

S: "I haven't a clue, Dad, but I feel sure that you're going to tell me."

D: "Of course, but you're going to help. Tell me what was Aaron's role amongst the Israelites?."

S: "Why, he was the first High Priest for the Israelites, wasn't he?"

D:"Yes, he was. And how did Paul describe Jesus in Hebrews 4? As a great High Priest. Listen to this: *"Therefore, since we have a great high priest who has gone through the heavens, Jesus the son of God, let us hold firmly to the faith we profess."*

S: "So we're actually getting two symmetries for the price of one?"

D: "You've got it!"

MY NAME IS OBADIAH – AND I'M SCARED TO DEATH

My name is Obadiah. I'm 32 years old, married. God has blessed me with four children. I'm a member of the

Sanhedrin. You probably know about the Sanhedrin. But it's worth going over the basics, just in case. The Sanhedrin is one of the pinnacles of the Jewish Establishment. We're treated with great respect even fear by those we oversee. That's not surprising because we have the power to inflict any punishment short of execution. Only the Roman authorities have that power. But we work closely with them. They leave us alone to get on with things and don't make many demands on us. As long as we toe the line we can usually get them to agree with what we want.

Being a member of the Sanhedrin is quite a position. We wear special robes, sit in the most important seats in the synagogues, take top table positions at meals, issue our interpretations of rules and regulations and so on. Also, although I wouldn't say this publicly, it's rather nice to be greeted with deference and respect when we walk around the city. It's also darned hard to become a member, so I really felt I had achieved my goal in life – until he came along.

I'm talking about Jesus. He made life difficult for us, for a short while, about three years. There's no doubt he was a prophet of sorts with the power to perform miracles of healing. We'd had John the Baptist but he came and went. After him we had to deal with this fellow. I think if he had stopped at miracles we wouldn't have minded but he didn't. He used to preach as well and what he preached got up our noses. He even slagged us off, accusing us of being hypocrites. Not only that, he said we were like white-washed tombs, clean on the outside, grimy inside. Worse still, he said that we actually prevented people from entering the kingdom of heaven. Us! And a lot more besides.

Well, we met as a Sanhedrin to discuss what we ought to do about him. There was a general consensus that it would be good if we could shut him up but, at that time, it was thought best to wait and see if his popularity died first. It had happened before , it could happen again. However, it didn't. Things got considerably worse.

MY NAME IS OBADIAH – AND I'M SCARED TO DEATH (2)

He actually started forgiving people for their sins. Now that's serious. Only God can do that. Jesus was saying that he was God! I am sure you understand. Clearly, that had to stop. You can't have everyone going around making that sort of claim. Where would that leave us, for goodness' sake? So we decided to take action but we needed to arrest Jesus when he didn't have his crowd of followers around. That was a stumbling block until we had a stroke of luck. One of Jesus' supporters came and told us he knew where we could find Jesus with just a few followers. It was up on the Mount of Olives.

So we sent a bevy of our soldiers and functionaries up there to arrest him and bring him back. They were able to do that. Then we set up a hastily convened court to try him. Looking back, I can see now that the trial was a bit of a farce. We didn't have any witnesses that made sense. They contradicted each other or just didn't really witness anything. Even Caiaphas, the High Priest, got fed up with it in the end. He jumped out of his chair and challenged Jesus straight out. *"I charge you under oath by the living God: tell us if you are the Christ, the Son of God."* Can you believe what Jesus replied? *"Yes, it is as you say"* Well, that obviously doomed him to death for blasphemy. But it's what he said next that has scared me to death. *"But I say to all of you: in the future you will see the Son of Man sitting at the right hand of the Mighty One and coming on the clouds of heaven.*

I didn't understand it at the time. None of us did. Frankly, I was blinded by hatred and anger that this nobody from the accursed north of the country could attack us, the Establishment, in the ways that he did. I wanted him dead. No doubt about that. I was so angry with the wretched man that I even jumped up myself and physically attacked him when he was blindfolded. I even asked him to prophesy who hit him.

Anyway, we took him off to Pontius Pilate, the Roman Governor, got a crowd together and forced Pilate to order his crucifixion. That suited us very well. I mean how could anyone who'd been sentenced to the most degrading and humiliating form of execution be seen as the Son of God?

MY NAME IS OBADIAH – AND I'M SCARED TO DEATH (3)

We took Jesus up to Golgotha where, to our immense satisfaction, he was crucified between two criminals.

We all taunted him. *"He saved others but he can't save himself"* and similar mocking shouts. It was there that things started to go wrong.

First of all the sky went dark and stayed that way for about three hours, even though there wasn't an eclipse. Then we got reports that the temple curtain had split in two. Then there was an earthquake. But even worse, quite a few tombs split open and we had reports that the people who had been buried there had had been raised to life. The guards at the crucifixions were plainly terrified and started exclaiming *"Surely he was the Son of God"*

I think we could have just about lived with that but the next thing that we knew all hell had broken loose. We'd had a guard put on the tomb where Jesus was buried and sealed it with a large stone. We also put a seal on it to emphasize the importance of not disturbing it. That was because we'd had reports that he'd said he would rise again on the third day. So we didn't want his followers stealing the body and claiming he was alive again.

We had just gone into our regular morning meeting, congratulating ourselves on dealing with the Jesus issue, when the chief guard appeared. Frankly, he looked in an awful state. Caiaphas made him sit down, handed him some water and asked him to report. This is what he said "At dawn this morning a couple of women who'd been at the crucifixion came to look at the tomb. Whilst we were getting ready to stop them from coming too near there was another earthquake – pretty violent. Then an angel appeared, rolled the stone away from the tomb and sat on it, right in front of our noses. He was huge. The only way I can explain his appearance was that it was as bright as lightning. His clothes were as white as snow. Putting it bluntly, we were scared to death and almost fainting with fright.

Then the angel spoke to the women *"Do not be afraid, for I know you are looking for Jesus, who was crucified. He is not here; he has risen, just as he said he would….. he has risen from the dead…"*

At that moment the cold fingers of fear settled on my heart and they're still there.

MY NAME IS OBADIAH – AND I'M SCARED TO DEATH (4)

I was feeling bad about what we'd done. However, things died down for a while, so I began to think I was worrying unnecessarily. Well, that time of relative peace came to an abrupt end.

We heard a strange noise, like a whirlwind, and sent a guard to investigate. What he told us set the alarm bells ringing again. Apparently followers of Jesus were preaching out in the open to a very large crowd – and in all sorts of different languages. How they managed to do that when most of them were born and raised in Galilee in the accursed, backward north of the country I do not know. But their preaching had some sort of impact because apparently about 3,000 of the crowd became followers of Jesus – based on the fact that he had risen from the dead! Why on earth did they believe that, when we had seen him die on the cross? I started to worry again – and with good reason.

You know that beggar that used to sit outside the temple pestering us every day? I was half convinced that he was faking it but the temple warden, who was a cousin of his and helped to put him there, assured me that he'd been crippled from birth. Anyway, as it happens, I had just asked the High Priest if we couldn't move him off somewhere well out of the way, when he comes hopping and skipping across the temple court on his own feet, accompanied by some of those wretched Galileans. The chief one was apparently called Peter and what he said scared me to death:

"You handed (Jesus) over to be killed, and you disowned him before Pilate, though he had decided to let him go. You disowned the Holy and Righteous One....You killed the author of life, but God raised him from the dead. We are witnesses of this.....It is Jesus' name and the faith that comes through him that has given this complete healing to (this man), as you can all see."

Well, we hauled them in and told them not to speak or preach at all in Jesus' name – or else it would be the worse for them. Did that stop them? No. They were at it again a few days later. So this time we had them flogged. What scared me most was that they actually looked happy about it and it didn't stop them from preaching. I wasn't sleeping at all well.

MY NAME IS OBADIAH –
AND I'M SCARED TO DEATH (5)

Look. The thing is, it was getting on my nerves. I was snapping at my wife and children. I didn't have much of an appetite. I couldn't concentrate in meetings. The High Priest was giving me curious glances. I couldn't sleep properly. Things weren't going well at all. I think I recognized that I'd been involved in something that was beyond my understanding. You know what? I think it was my pride and arrogance that were getting in the way. Well, how could I admit that we, the Sanhedrin, might have made a mistake and arranged the death a man who was, at the least a prophet? I had to do something about it or I felt I would go mad with fear.

The arresting team had discovered where the Galileans were staying. On a night when I couldn't sleep, I slipped out and found my way to their house. I had to bang on the door as they were all asleep. They ushered me in and the one I knew as Peter came into the room to greet me. You know what? I couldn't say anything. I was literally speechless. The next thing I knew I was on my face bawling my eyes out. I don't know how long I was down there but it felt like a long time. They didn't say anything but when I stopped they helped me to a chair and gave me a cup of wine. It was after that I found my voice but all I could say was "I'm sorry, I'm sorry, I'm sorry".

To make matters worse, Peter spoke: "You know that on the cross Jesus asked his Father to forgive you because you didn't know what you were doing? Well, that forgiveness extends to you now. You need to repent of the part you played in all of this and of all the wrong things you have done in your life. Then accept Jesus for whom he is, the Son of God. Will you do that?" I suddenly knew that he was right and that I needed to repent. I was also aware that I might never have another chance like this, so I did exactly that.

As soon as I did my fear evaporated. I felt an indescribable peace and joy. I was baptized and spent the night chatting with them. It suddenly all made sense. My final word on this subject is whatever you do, make sure you follow me to repentance and salvation.

A MOTHER REMINISCES

I think I was fourteen when I played my last games of jacks or hopscotch. That was just two years before it all started to happen. By then I was spending my days helping my mother in the house and vegetable garden and fetching water and doing laundry. Of course I knew I would be engaged to be married when I reached sixteen. My parents had already spoken to Joseph's parents, so it was clear something would happen. I was quite pleased really. Joseph was a decent hard-working man and I liked the look of him. Our engagement party was a lot of fun. Dad told some very funny jokes – a bit near the knuckle but nothing too untoward. Mum did all the baking. All my friends came.

It was only about two weeks after the party that things started to unravel in a big way. Mum realised she had left her shawl at Aunty Miriam's. As it was getting late and she had supper to prepare, she asked me if I would run over and fetch it for her. So off I trotted. I had just rounded the corner at the end of our street when, bang! I ran straight into this enormous man. He was huge, twice as tall as me. I had never seen him in our village before, so you can imagine how scared I was. I was getting ready to run away when he spoke to me. *"Greetings, you who are highly favoured, the Lord is with you."* Now what sort of greeting is that?

By that time I was quaking with fear, frozen to the spot, when he spoke again. *"Do not be afraid, Mary, you have found favour with God."* He actually knew my name! He said it in such a kind, warm voice that I stopped being afraid and wanted to ask him what he meant. Before I could he spoke again. That's when I thought he must have been a prophet or someone like that. *"You will be with child and give birth to a son, and you are to give him the name Jesus"* I assumed he was talking about my marriage to Joseph. So I was pleased that I would give Joseph a son. But then the man spoke again. *" He will be great and will be called the Son of the Most High."* Now, with all the will in the world, I knew he wasn't referring to Joseph. What he said next just made it more confusing.

He said *"The Lord God will give him the throne of his father David, and he will reign over the house of Jacob for ever; his kingdom will never end."* Now, what would you have thought if you had heard that? He was actually saying that my son would be a king, forever. I was going to be the mother of a king! There were just two problems. I was engaged to Joseph and I was a virgin. So how could this actually come about? Well, I asked him. He didn't bother with any of that. He just told me how I was to conceive. *"The Holy Spirit will come upon you, and the power of the Most High will overshadow you. So, the holy one to be born will be called the Son of God."* Do you realise what he was saying? I, me, was going to give birth to the Messiah!" Me!

A MOTHER REMINISCES (2)

Well, believe it or not, I had stopped being afraid and was totally calm at this point. It all seemed so unreal. I think I was remembering how the Lord spoke to Samuel when he was serving Eli at the temple. So I just said *"I am the Lord's servant. May it be to me as you have said."* Then he disappeared. So I turned round and then I bumped into my mother who had come out to see why I was taking so long. Needless to say, I had forgotten all about her shawl. She wasn't best pleased. I didn't tell her anything about my encounter.

It wasn't long afterwards that it happened. I was asleep in bed when I suddenly awoke to the most extraordinary sensation. It felt as if my whole body had come alive in a way I had never experienced before. The only way to describe it was to say that I was in rapture. I don't know how long the sensation lasted but it was nearly daylight before I fell asleep. Mum says that when she woke me I had a smile on my face.

A couple of months later I was sure. I was pregnant. At first my parents and Joseph were livid, as you can imagine. But then I told them about my meeting with this strange man, what he had said and what had happened afterwards. I am not sure that they believed everything I said, but at least they didn't throw me out. Instead I was bundled off to cousin Elizabeth, who's pregnant herself.

I did manage to have a heart to heart with Joseph before I left. He told me that he'd had it in mind to divorce me quietly. I wouldn't have blamed him if he had. But then he said he'd had a dream in which an angel said that he shouldn't be afraid to marry me. That I would conceive by the power of the Holy Spirit and would give birth to a son, to be called Jesus. Now my angel had told me that Jesus would be the Son of God. What he didn't tell me but what Joseph's angel told him was that Jesus would save his people from their sins. I can't say Joseph looked very happy about it but I could see he was sincere and I loved him for that. Anyway, he did marry me but we didn't sleep together until after Jesus had been born. However, I'm getting ahead of myself.

A MOTHER REMINISCES (3)

I get to cousin Elizabeth's where you'd expect that I would have to explain everything all over again. Not a bit of it. No sooner do I enter her house than Elizabeth says *"Blessed are you among women and blessed is the child you will bear. But why am I so favoured, that the mother of my Lord should come to me?"* Now what do you make of that? Elizabeth is a lot older than I am. The fact she's having a child at all is something of a miracle. I knew something remarkable had happened to me. It was then I began to realise that other people knew it too. I had no idea just how many of them there were.

On my return home Joseph and I started planning our wedding. We hadn't got very far when the village gets word that the Romans have ordered a census and we've all got to register in our home towns. As I'm pledged to be married to Joseph that means I have to go with him to his home town. So, after saying goodbye to my family we set off to cover the 70 odd miles to Bethlehem. We managed to fit in with a large group heading in the same direction, so our journey was uneventful, if not particularly comfortable.

When we got there I met all Joseph's relatives. I can't remember how long we stayed there but I do know that once I had given birth we had to keep Jesus in a manger because there wasn't anywhere else we could put him. Poor Joseph was totally in awe and still coming to terms with what had happened. I loved that baby so much. I expect all mothers say that! But I wonder how many mothers could match what happened subsequently. I'd only just recovered from the birth and got myself and Jesus sorted out when there were several loud bangs on the door. Joseph opened it and standing there were these scruffy-looking shepherds peering in.

Well, Joseph didn't want to let them in but the looks on their faces and what they said to him really left him with no alternative. It seemed that an angel – there were a lot of them about that night! – had appeared to them and told them that the Messiah – Christ the Lord was how he put it – had been born in Bethlehem and where to find him. Not content with that, a great company of the heavenly host had suddenly burst out of heaven, as if they couldn't be restrained, praising God and saying *"Glory to God…and peace to men on whom his favour rests."* So the shepherds had left their sheep to come and find this Saviour. With that, they burst into the room and gathered round the crib in awe and amazement. Then they rushed off repeating to anyone who cared to listen what they had told us.

A MOTHER REMINISCES (4)

What I can't remember is exactly when the wise men turned up. They had come from the east, looking for the King of the Jews . They were convinced that Jesus was him. They worshipped him and left us with gifts of gold, frankincense and myrrh. We subsequently learned that their visit to the "King of the Jews" had upset King Herod so they had gone home by a route that avoided him. It was all building up in a very special way but what I didn't know then was that the initial aspects of who Jesus was would come to a conclusion not in our village but in the great temple in Jerusalem. Nor would it happen with pomp and ceremony either. It would happen at the hands of two old people who were just about past it, a man and a woman - Simeon and Anna.

It happened like this. Forty days after the birth, we went to the temple to offer a sacrifice for my purification and to dedicate Jesus to the Lord. It wasn't a big deal, only about five miles. I hadn't been to Jerusalem very often and I loved all the bustle and noise and smells, particularly in the bazaar. But we had little time for all that, although Joseph did let me buy a few trinkets there. So we went on to the temple. How impressive it all looked and how clearly I see now that God's plan was unfolding. Unbeknown to us, whilst we were making our way to the temple, so was Simeon. There's not much I can tell you about him, except that he was old and, we subsequently learned, righteous and devout, which made what he had to say all the more meaningful.

Have you ever seen anyone acting under the prompting of the Holy Spirit. It's quite interesting. They do things that you wouldn't normally expect anyone to do. And that's what Simeon did. He came up to us and, to my astonishment, took Jesus out of my arms and held him. Then, looking up to heaven he praises God, and says:

"Lord, now let thy servant depart in peace, according to thy word, for mine eyes have seen thy salvation which thou hast prepared before the face of all people to be a light to the Gentiles and the glory of your people Israel."

Well, even though you would have thought we were getting used to the extraordinary, Joseph and I still marveled at these astonishing words. But that wasn't the end of it. Whilst I was basking in the immense favour God had placed on Joseph, me and Jesus, Simeon starts up again – and it's not good:

"This child is destined to cause the rising and falling of many in Israel, and to be a sign that will be spoken against, so that the thoughts of many hearts will be revealed. And a sword will pierce your own soul too."

I really didn't want to hear that! But, you know what? I put it behind me. I mean Jesus was only about a month and a half old. We had lots of years to spend watching him grow up, caring for him and enjoying his presence. Whilst I was thinking that, this woman comes up to us. Her name's Anna. She's eighty-four years old, she's a prophetess. First of all she gives thanks to God and then she starts talking to anyone who cares to listen about Jesus and how he was going to be the redemption of Jerusalem. I wasn't surprised. By now I was getting used to being told amazing things about Jesus. Already, stretching back we had had the visit of the angel, the virgin conception and birth, the shepherds and angels, the wise men and now Simeon and Anna. I kept it all close to my heart.

A MOTHER REMINISCES (5)

So we returned to Galilee and settled down, but not for long. Joseph comes in for breakfast with a troubled look on his face. "We've got to get out of here," he said. "An angel visited me last night and told me that Herod is going to search for us and kill Jesus. We've got to escape to Egypt." Egypt! Honestly! Since the angel told me I was going to give birth to Jesus I've had to stay with my aunt, travel to Bethlehem whilst almost full-term. Now we've got to go to Egypt. Where next, I wonder. So, off we go, saying farewell, yet again, to my parents who are looking more and more perplexed. Fortunately, my dad had some contacts in Egypt, so we made for them and settled down but expecting that we would return in due course, presumably when the angel said it would be safe for us, and, incidentally, fulfilling a prophecy by Hosea that "out of Egypt I called my son."

Whilst we were in Egypt we heard the terrible news that Herod had ordered the execution not just of every boy under two years living in Bethlehem but also all those in the surrounding area as well. You can understand why we went straight to Nazareth and by-passed Bethlehem. I mean how would you like to be the only mother in the town with a baby? So that's where Jesus grew up, in what we thought was a perfectly normal way. It was when he was twelve that we started to get an idea of how things were going to work out.

We had travelled to Jerusalem, as usual, for the Passover. So had hundreds of thousands of others. The place was noisy, cheerful and crowded. A large group of us had come, with our families. For the children it was a time of great excitement and fun, playing games with each other, buying treats, chasing after each other. We hardly saw anything of them from morning to dusk. So we weren't concerned when we realized that Jesus wasn't travelling home with us. We thought he was probably making his own way, with a group of friends. It was when he didn't turn up for the evening meal that we started to worry. First of all we went from one family to another looking for him but when we didn't find him we started to think that we might have left him behind. So we turned back and made our way to Jerusalem, filled with trepidation. I mean, how were we going to find him there, amongst so many people? Well, we spent three days scouring the city, getting more and more worried. Finally, we went back to the temple and there he was, not the slightest bit concerned! The odd thing was that he was surrounded by the teachers of the law and discussing things with them. We could see that they were amazed at his understanding and the questions he was asking. I mean, he was only twelve, for goodness' sake.

I rushed over to him. I was so relieved I got cross. I can still remember what I said: "Son, why have you treated us like this? We've been all over the city looking for you!" Do you know what he said? "Didn't you know I had to be in my Father's house?" Well, Joseph was a bit put out by that and I didn't understand either. So we pulled him out of there and took him home. The atmosphere was a bit frosty to start with but, as I recalled all the strange events leading up to his birth and particularly what the angel had said to me, I began to realize that our relationship was going to have its unusual elements, to say the least. And so it proved. Yes, he was obedient to us but, as he grew up, his wisdom became apparent to all, as did his godliness.

A MOTHER REMINISCES (6)

Well, you know about as much as I do from there on. You know about his temptation, his baptism, how he chose his disciples and his ministry of teaching and healing and miracles. The only worry we had, and it was a major one was the way he was getting up the noses of establishment. The thing is, he hadn't had any proper training. He hadn't studied under the teachers of the law or become a member of the Pharisees. He was outside the establishment and, worse, he spent a lot of time disputing with them. We kept getting word back that they were getting really angry with him. So much so, that we started worrying for his well-being. We were afraid that they would throw him into prison, or worse, to shut him up.

We didn't expect that they would crucify him for blasphemy! Couldn't they see that he was the Messiah? Far from it! It was his declaration that he was the Son of God that gave them the chance to eliminate him. I personally think it was the realization that their whole way of life was under threat that led them to put him to death in the cruelest way imaginable. Even I could hardly recognize him as they led him out to the crucifixion site. His face was a mess. His back had been ripped apart. There was blood flowing down from his head. It tore my heart apart. I could hardly bring myself to follow him to the site. I felt every hammer blow as they nailed him to the cross.

Don't you think it was extraordinary that, as he hung there in agony, he still found the strength to tell John to look after me? So, sobbing my heart out I went back with John to where he was staying. You know how it took us three days to find Jesus at the temple? Well, it was also three days after the crucifixion that rumours began to spread that Jesus had been seen alive. First, John told me he had been to the tomb and it was empty. Then he told me that Jesus had met with the disciples. Finally, Jesus appeared to five hundred of us – and to me. I won't tell you what he said but I know now that I will be with him in heaven, in glory and that my name will be honoured throughout the world. I am content.

THE RIGHT WAY AND THE WRONG WAY

1 Kings 12
Acts 14

The reading for June 23 in the "Through the Bible in a Year" Bible covers two stories, one from the Old Testament and one from the New Testament. Together they are a lesson in how to do things the right way and the wrong way.

Rehoboam has succeeded his father, Solomon, as King. Relations between Judah and the ten tribes that make up Israel have been fractious. Now the leaders of the ten tribes come to Rehoboam. They complain that King Solomon *"put a heavy yoke on us, but now lighten the harsh labour and heavy yoke he put on us and we will serve you."* Rehoboam says *"Come back in three days and I will answer you."* This gives Rehoboam time to consult with two groups of people. First he consults the elders who served his father. They tell him that, *"if you will be a servant to these people and serve them and give them a favourable answer they will always be your servants."*

Then Rehoboam consults the young men who grew up with him. They tell him to say, *"My father laid on you a heavy yoke; I will make it even heavier. My father scourged you with whips; I will scourge you with scorpions."* Rehoboam follows the advice of the young men. Is it any surprise that the ten tribes reject him as king and go their separate way?

In the New Testament, the elders of the early church are grappling with a problem that has arisen in Antioch. Jewish members of the church are insisting that Gentile members should conform to Jewish law and be circumcised. A council meeting is held. Following that a letter is written to: *"The Gentile believers in Antioch, Syria and Cilicia (part of Turkey). We have heard that some went out without our authority and disturbed you, troubling your minds by what they said….It seemed good to the Holy Spirit and to us not to burden you with anything beyond the following requirements: You are to abstain from food sacrificed to idols, from blood, from the meat of strangled animals and from sexual immorality. You will do well to avoid these things. Farewell."* The Antioch church was glad for the encouraging message.

Can you spot a vital difference between the two stories? In the first there was plenty of consultation, but not with God. In the second, the Council at Jerusalem did consult God. *"It seemed good to the Holy Spirit and to us."* God took priority.

SO WHAT'S GOING ON?

Brother: "Look Jacob. Rebecca has asked me to have a word with you. She's worried and so am I. The thing is you've stopped going regularly to the synagogue. And when you do go all you can talk about is this chap Jesus as if he was God or something. In fact, that's all you seem to talk about now. You know as well as I do that he was crucified as a criminal. If you keep that up you're going to get slung out on your ear. Not only that, but I've heard that steps are going to be taken to exclude you from our town square meetings. It all started when you returned from going to the Passover in Jerusalem. And we're getting the same reports about Joseph, who went on the trip with you. So what's going on?"

Jacob: "The thing is, Isaac, I just don't know. I'll try to explain. I went off to Jerusalem for the Passover, as you say. I was really enjoying the trip. I spent time with family. We had some good meals and celebrations. I was able to conduct some good business deals. I even managed to sell off that bit of land we couldn't do anything with. We went to worship at the temple where I managed to have a chat with our cousin Saul. You know, the one who serves in the Holy of Holies.

Anyway, Joseph and I were wandering around the market place looking for trinkets to bring back for our wives when we heard this extraordinary sound. It was like nothing I've ever heard before or since – a sort of howling gale out of a clear blue sky. It was over in a flash. I thought "What was that!" So did everyone else. So we ran to where we thought the noise came from. Quite a crowd gathered. There must have been, I don't know, three or four thousand of us.

For several minutes there was nothing to see but then a bunch of men pour out of a house and start yelling and screaming and jumping up and down. I couldn't understand what most of them were saying as they were speaking in foreign languages or something. As I could tell they were from Galilee I thought it was their accent I couldn't make out. But some guy standing near me told me that at least one of them was speaking Persian. Anyway, this guy steps forward, calls for quiet and says….."

SO WHAT'S GOING ON? (2)

"We're not drunk. It's far too early for that. What's just happened is what the Prophet Joel prophesied. He said," *I will pour out my Spirit on all people*".

Now you have to understand that I wasn't making notes or anything, so I may not have got it all exactly but I can remember the gist of what he said. He starts talking about Jesus. He tells us that he was a man *"accredited to us by God by miracles, wonders and signs, as you yourselves know."* Well, I didn't know although I had heard rumours whilst staying in Jerusalem. But I was wondering why, if that was the case, he'd been crucified as a criminal.

It was almost as though this chap, apparently called Peter, was reading my mind because he tells us that Jesus was handed over by *"God's set purpose and foreknowledge"* to be put to death by crucifixion. Well, I'd already heard he'd been crucified, so that was nothing new. But what he said next amazed me. He said that *"God raised him to life"* and that we, by which I presumed he meant himself and the men with him, were witnesses to that, by which I presumed he meant they'd seen him alive again. He then said *"God has made this Jesus, whom you crucified, both Lord and Christ."*

Clearly, a lot of people around me knew what he was talking about because they were really messed up. They asked Peter "What shall we do?" He said "Repent and be baptised." Well, I didn't help to get him crucified, so I stood there watching. Thousands of them got on their knees and repented. It was weird seeing so many do that.

While I was watching them Peter was working his way through the crowd and he gets to me. When I look at him, all I can say is that it was as though a light went off in my mind. Suddenly, I don't know how, I just knew Jesus really was Lord and Christ and that he'd come back to life. Never mind what sort of death he died, I knew that he wanted to be lord of my life and give me life in a new way. So I got on my knees, repented of all I'd done wrong and got prayed for. Now I'm a new man and Jesus is my Lord. And, Isaac, if you've got any sense you'll make him Lord of your life too.

YES, I MET HIM

Acts 9

We had been waiting since dawn. We knew they were coming and didn't want to miss them. Jacob had just come back from visiting the city. He'd met them, heard Paul speak and heard their plans for the next part of their trip. We were on their route.

It was a glorious morning. The sky was a cloudless, brilliant blue. The sun was ablaze and high in the sky. It was another hot day. The sea seemed full of crystals shimmering and flashing white, dazzling our eyes. "There they are!" someone said and we peered into the distance. A small group of men were emerging from the haze on the brow of the hill, the dust rising from their feet. We gathered together across the track. On they came. Jacob went out to meet them.

"Which one is Paul?" we asked. Jacob had to point him out. He was the small one, with somewhat bandy legs, rather bald and a prominent nose. But it was none of those that caught our attention. It was his eyes. They seemed to look into us, through us and up to eternity. We gasped when he raised the jug of water to his lips. His robe slipped back and we could see welts from the floggings he'd received.

We knew much. We'd heard that Jesus was the Messiah, that he'd sacrificed his own life to save ours, that he'd risen from the dead to show that Satan had no hold on him. We had declared ourselves to be his followers. Now we had the chance to hear from someone who had actually met him, who'd sacrificed his own luxurious lifestyle to live a life of hardship and suffering as a follower of Jesus and who could give us teaching on the way we should live. The excitement was intense. All thoughts of thirst and hunger died away. We crowded round, offering the bread, cheese, wine, grapes and raisins that we'd brought.

Jacob introduced Paul to each one of us. Then we met Luke and the other members of his small party. When Paul got to me he looked at me and it was as though a shock went through my heart. We heard stories of the towns and cities they had been through and the successes, trials and tribulations they had experienced. Our hearts swelled to think that we were face to face with an apostle and his followers.

Paul stepped into the middle of the group. "Yes", he began "I met him......."

AN INTERVIEW WITH PAUL

Interviewer "Thank you being with us tonight, Paul, and making room in your busy schedule. I'm just sorry there aren't more of us here to listen to you."

Paul: "Oh, don't worry about that! I'd far rather be with twenty followers of Jesus who are on fire than a hall full of luke-warms."

I: Well, I've got a set of questions I'd like to ask. The first is "How did you become a Christian?"

P: "That's an easy one to answer. I was on my way to Damascus to seek out and imprison Christians when Jesus met me. As far as I knew we'd put him to death but there he was. It blew my mind and, from then on, I followed him with all my heart and strength."

I: Well, that's certainly an unusual way to start your Christian life. So, what were you like before you became a Christian?"

P: "You've caught me on a sore spot there. I was awful. I thought I was doing ok. I mean I was a full-blooded Jew, studying at the feet of Gamaliel. I knew, like we all did, that we'd screwed up in the past by worshipping gods other than Jehovah. So I set out in a major way to be as good a Jew as I possibly could. Obeying every precept you could come across. I wouldn't have been sitting here talking with you like this, for example. You were a sinner and I was a Jew and proud of it. Talk about religious. I'd have won a prize. Actually, I think I may have done!"

I: "And what are you like now you are a Christian?"

P: "I would like to think that I am a totally changed person. Humility would be the first word to come to mind. Humbled by the fact that the Son of God, no less, died for me – and you. Humbled by the fact that he took me from a wretched and angry life to one of peace and contentment, irrespective of the circumstances. And then privileged because he made me an apostle and allowed me to preach the Gospel just about everywhere – even here."

I: "Finally, what would you say to someone who was thinking of becoming a Christian?"

P: "I urge that person to take that step of faith. Listen to those who have already done so. Believe what you read in the Bible. Place yourself in the hands of Jesus. He won't let you down and glory awaits."

WHY DID YOU DO IT, PAUL?

Interviewer: Well, Paul, we've known each other for many years. You're now in Rome awaiting a trial from which you have little hope of emerging with your life. Looking back, shouldn't you be asking yourself "Why did I do it?" I mean you had everything going for you. You were raised in a fine Jewish family, doing very well in Tarsus. You were a Roman citizen – and that's not to be sneezed at. Your parents sent you to Rome to study under Gamaliel, one of the finest Rabbis of the age. I think you had got to the point where you either had been or were on the verge of being admitted to the Sanhedrin, the top council. You were certainly their hatchet man when it came to sorting out followers of Jesus and a fine job you were making of that. You weren't short of money. Then what happened?

Paul: Everything you say is right. That's exactly the person I was….until that fateful day on the road to Damascus. I was going there, as I think you know, to arrest more followers of Jesus and throw them into prison. Like you, I considered Jesus to be an impostor and a danger to the pure Jewish faith we all grew up with and supported. All the talk by his followers of his coming back from the dead was just a load of rubbish that I had no time for. Until I met Jesus myself. I'm not fooling. I actually met him. Just the once. On the road to Damascus.

I was hit by a bright light and fell to the ground. Then I heard a voice. It said "Saul", that was my name then, "Saul, why do you persecute me?" Well, I hadn't a clue who was talking to me and the light was so bright I couldn't see anything. So, I asked who it was. Can you imagine how dumbfounded I was when the voice said *"I am Jesus whom you are persecuting."*

Well, that was it. I knew we had crucified him, so what was he doing on the road to Damascus? Then I remembered the words of his disciples, Peter and John, who swore blind in front of the Sanhedrin that Jesus had come back from the dead and were actually happy that we flogged them for telling everyone so. Now here he was. It gave me the most awful shock. That's when I realised that what they'd said was true and it changed my life.

SYMMETRY - TEMPLES

On the way to the Promised Land God gives Moses instructions as to how the nation is to live and the laws and regulations to abide by.

The most serious of these laws tells them they must *"have no other gods before me."* Well, a lot of the Old Testament is taken up with the trials and tribulations of a nation that fails to keep its laws, particularly the one mentioned. But, for our purposes we need to take a look at King David. He is fully entrenched on the throne of Israel and has it in mind to build a temple for God. However, Nathan the prophet tells David that he is not the one to build a temple. It will be Solomon, David's son by Bathsheba, who will build it.

And so it proves. Solomon has a magnificent temple built and God comes to establish his presence there. As the Old Testament tells us: *"The priests could not perform their service (*because a cloud had filled the temple) *for the glory of the Lord filled his temple."* Then God speaks to Solomon *"I have consecrated this temple… by putting my name there forever. My eyes and heart will always be there."* However, God goes on to say that if Solomon or his sons turn away from him *"then I will cut off Israel from the land…and will reject this temple…"*

And so it proves. By worshipping other gods, Israel is doomed to destruction and exile and the temple is destroyed. God has left.

So where's the symmetry between the temples in the Old Testament and New?

Paul gives us a clue when he visits Athens and speaks to the members of the Areopagus. *"….the Lord of heaven and earth does not live in temples built by hands….in him we live and move and have our being."* With the advent of Jesus who opened the way for each one of us to have a living relationship with God we now know that God lives in us. There is no longer a physical building. We are his living temples. But the same rules apply. If we no longer serve the living God but exchange his glory for other images, if we exchange the truth of God for a lie and worship and serve created things, if we fail to retain the knowledge of God and go our own ways, doing things that ought not to be done then God gives us over and leaves us to go to our judgment. Don't be like Israel.

CAPTAINS' TALES

Acts 27,8

Captain 1 We were just about to set sail for Asia when this centurion turned up with a bunch of sorry-looking prisoners. Needless to say he commandeered space we could ill afford but you can't argue with the might of Rome, can you? I had a bad feeling about it. I don't like carrying prisoners at the best of times. You can't trust them and they're just as likely to slit your throat, given half a chance. So we land at Sidon and, to my astonishment, the centurion lets one of the prisoners called Paul off the boat apparently to visit some friends. What sort of prisoner is that? I imagined we wouldn't see him again but he duly turned up and off we set. Anyway, I was glad to see the back of them when they got off at Myra.

Captain 2 Mine was a much larger and stronger boat than his. So I didn't mind taking on some extra hands. Now I think about it I should have listened to the crew. They reckoned it was bad luck to take on the prisoners. Anyway, it was more profit for me. It should have been plain sailing to Italy but things went badly wrong.

Perhaps I was somewhat premature in welcoming the centurion and his motley crew on board.

We had to sail round the lee of Crete. Whilst we were doing that this prisoner, Paul, tells his centurion that the voyage is doomed. Goodness only knows how he knew better than me what was what, although, to be frank, I did have my eye on the profit. So we sailed on. We thought we'd make harbour for the winter but were blown into the mother and father of all storms.

It got so bad we not only had to lighten the vessel by throwing our cargo and tackle overboard but we also had to sling ropes underneath to hold the vessel together. I hadn't a clue where we were as we couldn't see any stars. Then, this bloke Paul pipes up again and do you know what he says? "You should have taken my advice." Fat lot of help that was! He then goes on to say that none of us will be lost even though the ship will. So bang goes my profit! He then tells us that we are going to run aground somewhere.

Well, after fourteen days that's just what happened. I don't want to see Paul or any other prisoner ever again.

I WAS A MEMBER OF THE PRAETORIAN GUARD

Ephesians 6:20

Day 1
Wife: "Flavius, you look really smart in your new Praetorian Guard uniform. Let me just take that piece of fluff off your tunic."

Husband "A pretty penny it's all cost us. But don't worry, I'll get it back in pay and bonuses and, of course, all the protection money I can extract from those accursed Christians that seem to be spreading across Rome like wildfire. I wonder what my first task will be. Can't wait to find out."

W: "Well have a good day. I look forward to hearing how it goes."

Day 2

W: "What a rotten job they've given you, having to guard a prisoner, and a Christian to boot. You say you're actually chained to him for the whole day? That's awful."

H: "Don't worry dear. I don't like it much myself but, you know what? It goes with the territory. I'm the new boy on the campus so I'm bound to get the job no-one wants. I'll be able to pass it on to the next recruit that comes along. Now, where's that polish you bought? I need to stay smart. Can't afford to let the others down, can I?"

Day 3

H: It's really odd. I've been guarding this man for three days now and I actually quite like him. His name's Paul. He's very bright, funny, cracks lots of jokes and talks twenty to the dozen. Also, and this is the best part, you won't believe how many people come in to see and chat with him and they bring him all sorts of things – food, clothes, bedding. You name it, anything to make him comfortable. What's more, I get to share them. So don't worry about supper. I can't eat another thing."

W: "Listen. You're not getting too chummy with him, are you? You've only been there three days. I don't want you to blot your copybook. What will the others think? You'll be putting yourself in terrible danger if you do."

Day 4
H: "I couldn't help it. What he said makes absolute sense. I now know that there is a real God and that he sent his son Jesus to save us from our sins. I've accepted him as my Lord and Saviour and, yes, if you want to put it that way, I've become a Christian.
W: "Oh, for goodness' sake!"

Day 5
Centurion: "Are you Flavius' wife?"
W: "Yes"
C: "We executed him today for being a Christian. Here are his belongings."

DID GOD CAUSE THE DESTRUCTION OF THE TEMPLE?

In AD70 the Romans came, besieged and captured Jerusalem destroying the temple. Jesus told us it was going to happen but the interesting question is "Did God have a hand in it?" I think he might have done. Here's why.

The first question is "Is this the sort of terrible behaviour that God would allow?" Over to you, Jeremiah the prophet. The Babylonians invaded Edom, Moab, Ammon, Tyre, Sidon and Judah. In BC586 they captured Jerusalem. Jeremiah foresaw this. *I will hand all your countries over to my servant Nebuchadnezzar, king of Babylon.* Did you read that right? His servant? God was using Nebuchadnezzar to achieve his ends, including the destruction of Jerusalem. How sad that he turned against his own people. Do you know why? Because they forsook him and worshipped other gods. Is there a lesson for us there?

Let's take a look at the key event leading up to the AD70 destruction of the temple. Something curious happened when Jesus, God's son, was crucified. The bible tells us that *"When Jesus had cried out again in a loud voice, he gave up his spirit. At that moment the curtain of the temple was torn in two."* Now why on earth should that have happened? It was some distance away from the crucifixion site. The explanation given in the New International Version Study Bible is that *"It was the inner curtain that separated the Holy Place from the Most Holy Place. The tearing of the curtain signified Christ's making it possible for believers to go directly into God's presence."*

On the face of it, what might have seemed a minor matter was hugely, religiously significant. If a believer could go straight to God through Jesus, then what was the point of all the priestly set up, the sacrifices, the ark, the fine robes, the Holy and Most Holy places? Perhaps God was telling us that there was no point whatsoever and that the temple was no longer relevant.

If that was the case, the Israelites hadn't got the message. First of all, the establishment failed to recognise Jesus as the son of God. So, no doubt they either replaced or repaired the curtain. Then they set about persecuting Jesus' followers, even going so far as Damascus with the intention of throwing them into prison. If the Jews had had their way, Christianity would have been stifled at birth. Something had to happen. In my view that something was God's servants, the Romans.

A HIGH PRIEST REMINISCES

Reporter: "Thank you, Caiaphas, for agreeing to this interview. You don't mind if I take notes, do you?"

C: "No, by all means. I am a very old man now and would like to leave an accurate account of my time as High Priest and afterwards."

R: "So, looking back over your momentous time in office and the years since, would you say that the destruction of the temple by the Romans in the year 3830 (AD70) was the most significant event of your involvement with the establishment?"

C: "Well, it certainly was a terrible time and not just for our temple worship but also for our race. Over 1 million of us died at that time, you know. But, having spent years mulling it over I have, somewhat reluctantly, I might say, come to the conclusion that the appalling death and disaster of AD70 might just be outweighed by the death of just one man."

R: "I'm sorry. I don't follow."

C: "No, it's been some time since he was put to death but I wonder if we didn't make a terrible mistake. I am talking about Jesus of Nazareth. We hated him at the time. By we, I mean the priests, council leaders, Pharisees and teachers of the law – in other words, the establishment. He came preaching a way of life that was totally contrary to all we had sought to establish. Although I didn't see any myself, I was told that he performed extraordinary miracles of healing. If he had left it at that I am sure we would have given him the honour due to a prophet. Actually, that's not true. We didn't treat our prophets very well either.

What got up our noses was his preaching. It seemed that he saw us as obstacles to the Kingdom of God. Us! I won't go into the details of it all but I do remember when we put him on trial. We asked him straight out *"Are you, then, the Son of God?"* He looked straight at me and his answer burned its way into my heart. *"You are right in saying that I am"* You, of course, know, being a devout Jew, that "I am" is how God describes himself. I was thunderstruck. But I couldn't do anything because I was carried along by the wave of fury that enveloped the trial. So we sent him to Pilate for crucifixion. Since then I have always wondered. I think he might just have been who he said he was."

AN IINTERVIEW WITH POLYCARP

Interviewer: "You're Bishop of Smyrna. It's clear that the authorities are coming after you. They've arrested just about everyone else. So, before you go to your doom will you give me some views about your faith, for the record. Is that alright?"

Polycarp: "By all means."

I: "Good. Let's start at the beginning. What's a Christian?"

P: A Christian is someone who follows Jesus Christ. In other words, accepts that Jesus was who he said he was, the Son of God. He came to reveal God's majesty and authority to us through the miracles he performed and his teaching. But, perhaps more important than that, he made it clear he had come to die in our place and, in so doing, take away the sins of those who put their trust in him. So we, who follow Jesus have faith that we have been made holy by his death and will join him in heaven once we die. We have this confirmed by the fact that Jesus conquered death and rose from the grave. We will do the same."

I: "But how do you know all this? I mean, here we are in AD156 and what you're talking about happened over 120 years ago? Is it possible that you're deluded?"

P: "Well, I've been a follower of Jesus for 86 years. So it was in AD70 that I made my confession of faith and committed my life to him. That was only 40 years after Jesus'crucifixion. At that time there were many around who had witnessed his death and resurrection and would willingly speak of it. Also, I was a student of John's. As you know, he was very close to Jesus. He died around the turn of the century. No, there's no delusion here."

I: I think I can see the arresting officer and his squadron approaching. Can you quickly tell me what you mean by a "confession of faith"?"

P: "There's no need to rush. I'm over 90, so I'm not going anywhere fast! A confession of faith starts with the recognition that your life up to that point has not been one of placing God at its centre and giving him the glory he deserves. You are sorry for that. You recognize that Jesus came to point this out to you and to die in your place. You acknowledge that Jesus is the Son of God and you commit yourself to follow him for the rest of your days."

I:"Thanks. I'd better go now. They're at the door."

A DIFFERENT INTERVIEW WITH POLYCARP*

(In the arena at Smyrna)

Proconsul: "What is wrong with saying "Lord" and "Caesar" and sacrificing ... and thereby saving your life?"

Polycarp: "I am not willing to do what you advise me."

Pro: "Consider your great age. Swear by the genius of Caesar.... Say "Away with the atheists... Swear and I will release you. Curse Christ."

Pol: "Eighty-six years have I served him, and he has never done me any harm. How could I blaspheme my King and Saviour? I am a Christian. If you are willing to learn what Christianity is, set a time at which you can hear me."

Pro: "Try to persuade the people."

Pol: "You I consider worthy...for we have been taught to pay respect to governments and authorities appointed by God as long as it does us no harm. But, ...I do not consider them worthy of my defence."

Pro: "I have wild beasts. I shall have you thrown before them...."

Pol: "Let them come. It is out of the question for us to change from the better to the worse, but the opposite is worthy of honour: to turn around from evil to justice."

Pro: "If you belittle the beasts and do not change your mind, I shall have you thrown into the fire."

Pol: "You threaten me with a fire that burns but for an hour and goes out after a short time, for you do not know the fire of the coming judgment and of eternal punishment for the godless. Why do you wait? Bring on whatever you will."

As Polycarp spoke these and similar words, he was full of courage and joy. His face shone with inward light. He was not in the least disconcerted by all these threats. The Proconsul was astounded. Three times he sent his herald to announce in the midst of the arena, "Polycarp has confessed that he is a Christian"

No sooner was this announced than the whole multitude, both pagans and Jews, yelled with uncontrolled anger at the top of their voices, "He is the teacher of Asia! The father of the Christians: The destroyer of our gods! He has persuaded many not to sacrifice and not to worship."

The fuel for the pyre was very quickly piled around him. They wanted to fasten him with nails. "Let me be. He who gives me strength to endure the fire will also give me the strength to remain at the stake unflinching...." When he had spoken the Amen and finished his prayer the executioners lit the fire.

---

* *Extracts from the Martyrdom of the Holy Polycarp, written on 22 February, 156*

SOME MORE ARTICLES

WHY DIDN'T HE ASK THE RIGHT QUESTION?

Have you ever come out of a "meeting" with someone then, seconds later, thought of exactly the right words to say and wished you'd thought of them earlier? I think that must have happened to Nicodemus.

He'd heard about Jesus and all the things he was doing across Israel – healing, teaching and preaching. So he decides to visit him. He comes at night. He calls Jesus "Rabbi". He knows Jesus is a teacher who's come from God. So here he has someone who can answer all the right questions. But when Jesus tells him *"No-one can enter the Kingdom of God unless he is born again."* Nicodemus gets totally confused as to how anyone can enter his mother's womb a second time. Jesus gives him a helping hand *"No-one can enter the Kingdom of God unless he is born of water and the Sprit."* Nicodemus is floundering. "How can this be?" he asks. Jesus is somewhat indignant. *"You are Israel's teacher and you do not understand these things?"*

What might Jesus have said if Nicodemus had asked the right question? Who knows, but here's one possibility.

In John's Gospel we learn that God is spirit. Whilst in the Garden of Eden, Adam and Eve had been able to relate to God directly, that is spiritually. They could see him, talk to him, walk with him on a daily basis - and hide from him. When Adam and Eve were kicked out of the Garden of Eden that spirit died in them. As a result, that wonderful relationship died as well. So, in order to restore that relationship we need to be spiritually reborn.

So, the question is "How do we get back the Spirit that enables us to relate once again with our God?" The answer is to ask. And this is how it happens. First of all we acknowledge that we are sinners, steeped in sin. We recognise that we can't remove that sin by our own efforts, no matter how hard we try. Only Jesus can remove our sin from us. He made that possible by dying on the cross and paying the price for our sins. We confess to him that we are sinners and thank him for his sacrifice on our behalf. We commit ourselves to follow him for the rest of our lives, living in accordance with his teachings. We ask to be filled with the Holy Spirit, are baptised, reborn and enter the kingdom of God. Let's make sure we ask the right question.

WHY ARE CHRISTIANS PERSECUTED?

In no less than 50 countries in the world Christians suffer from persecution. It's not all out war but it's sporadic, localised, widespread and inexorable.

In Pakistan there are "blasphemy" laws. These prescribe the death penalty for "defiling the name of Mohammed".

They are often used against Christians to settle personal grievances. A 12 year old Christian girl with Down's syndrome is charged with burning the Koran which carries the death penalty. It now appears that a local mullah was allegedly seen stuffing burnt pages into her bag. A 13 year old Christian girl was drugged and raped by three men. A month later one of the accused burst into her family home with five other men and beat the family up, causing a pregnant woman to give birth to two stillborn babies. The police refused to register the rapes and declared one of the accused, a retired police inspector's son, innocent.

In Sri Lanka a Christian boy was beaten by a Buddhist monk and left bleeding from his ear when he professed his faith in the classroom.

In Egypt an affray between Muslims and Christians, in which two Muslims and two Christians were killed, 10 Christians hospitalised and scores of homes and businesses belonging to Christians looted and torched, resulted in the 12 Christian men charged being sentenced to life imprisonment whilst 8 Muslims were acquitted.

In India a church leader and twelve families in his congregation were attacked by Hindu extremists. The leader was seriously injured. Around 50 Hindus then attacked the whole Christian community, injuring 20, tearing clothes off some of the women and looting homes.

Believe me, these are a only a minute fraction of the "incidents" that impacted Christians during the last year, as reported by the International Barnabas Fund which supports Christians in distress.

Why is it that there is such persecution when the essence of our faith is to love our neighbour and to live peaceably with everyone? There are more reasons but two things stand out. The first is that the crusades and the appalling manner in which they were pursued left an indelible impact on the Middle East and, hence, Muslims. The second is that, in many countries that were former colonies of the West and some that were not, Christianity is associated with the colonialism of the past and the political and military objectives of the present decadent West.

What can we do to help our persecuted brothers and sisters? We can start by praying. You do pray, don't you?

TIME FOR A SPIRITUAL HEALTH CHECK?

Son: " Our Youth Leader challenged us to produce a spiritual health checklist and find a guinea pig to try it on. Will you help?"
Dad: "I'll give it a go. It's not too strenuous, is it?"
S: "I don't know. I've only just put it together. Here goes. Did you read your bible today and, if so, for how long and what did you read?"
D:"That's easy. Yes, I did read it. I suppose it must have been for about five minutes and I read a couple of psalms. Now let's see. Which ones were they? Hmmm. No. Sorry. I can't remember which they were.

S: "Right. Next question. Did you pray today. If so, what about and for how long did you pray?"

D: "Well, that's pretty easy too. I certainly prayed. I'd put my car keys down somewhere and was blowed if I could remember where. I was in danger of missing the train when the thought came into my head that they were on the shelf in the kitchen. That's where I found them. I guess I must have prayed for about ten seconds. It's great, isn't it? Answered prayer, I mean. I really ought to do it more often."

S: "Next question. Did you go to church last Sunday and what did you put in the collection?"

D: "Well, I did go. I got a dirty look from the Vicar for coming in after the first hymn. What did I put in the collection? Fortunately I had a couple of £2 coins in my pocket, so I put those in. I'm enjoying this."

S: "It gets a bit tougher now. Are you aware of any poor people in our parish and what are you doing to help them?"

D: "I guess there are some, probably on the council estate. I haven't met any of them personally and I'm not doing anything myself to help them but I feel sure the church must be doing something."

S: "OK. Next question. Are you doing anything to support the church's activities?"

D: "Oh yes, I turn out once a year to clean up the parking area. Oh, and Mum helps with the flowers.

S: "No dad. I mean are you involved in anything like a house group or bible study group or an outreach group."

D: Good grief, no! I haven't got time for any of that stuff. Anyway I leave that sort of thing to the Vicar. You know what? I'm not really enjoying this anymore.

WHAT WAS THE POINT OF ISRAEL?

Son: "Dad, I would like to know, what was the point of Israel?"

Father: "What do you mean, son?"

S: "Well, I have just finished reading that part of the Old Testament which covers the history of Israel. It's a disaster story. I mean, God promises Abraham that he will make his descendants into a great nation and that all peoples on earth will be blessed through him. So we get the story of how Abraham's family becomes a tribe that grows into a nation that takes over the Promised Land. So far so good.

But once they're in the Promised Land, Israel, it all goes pear-shaped. They forsake God, worship other gods, in fact, behave as badly as the nations driven out before them. They totally ignore the warnings given by God and the prophets about what will happen if they do that. The net result is that their cities are destroyed, the people taken into exile and the land ravaged and occupied by others. Even after they return from exile they are subjected to foreign rule – Persians, Greeks and Romans. Not content with that, they try to wipe out Christianity before it's even got going. Then along come the Muslims and the Jews only get back some form of independence in the 20th century. So I ask you again, "What was the point of Israel? And doesn't it show God up in a bad light that his plan went so wrong?"

D: "If you look at the surface facts, it's all a huge mistake. But you need to look a little deeper into what's going on.

Everything in the Bible hinges on Jesus. Everything that goes before him in a sense prepares the way; everything that comes after him is impacted by him. What do I mean? Through Israel God makes it clear to us that we are not capable of managing our own destiny. What God said about Israel, in effect, was "If you live by the laws and regulations I set before you, you will be a holy nation." They just couldn't do it. Yes, they tried time and time again but it always ended up badly.

So what's the message for us? The people of Israel couldn't be holy through their own efforts, nor can we. We need something more or, as the Bible tells us, we need someone to help us. That someone is Jesus, God's son. God sent him to make us holy. We can learn a lot from Israel."

WHY ARE THINGS GOING WRONG?

Ben Stein, a presenter for the American TV network, NBC, apparently wrote this. It could equally apply here in the UK:

"I am a Jew and every single one of my ancestors was Jewish. It doesn't bother me when people call those beautiful lit up trees, Christmas trees. I don't feel threatened. I don't feel discriminated against. That's what they are, Christmas trees.

It doesn't bother me when people say "Merry Christmas". They're not slighting me or getting ready to put me in a ghetto. Actually I kind of like it. It shows we are all brothers and sisters celebrating this happy time of year. I don't like being pushed around for being a Jew and I don't think Christians like being pushed around for being Christians. I think people who believe in God are sick and tired of getting pushed around, period.

In any case, where did the idea come from that we should worship celebrities and we're not allowed to worship God? There are a lot of us who are wondering where these celebrities came from and where the America we knew went to.

Billy Graham's daughter, Anne, was interviewed and was asked "How could God let something like Hurricane Katrina (which had a devastating effect on New Orleans) happen? She replied, "I believe God is deeply saddened by this, just as we are, but for years we've been telling God to get out of our schools, to get out of our government, to get out of our lives. Being the gentleman he is, I believe he has calmly backed out. How can we expect God to give us his blessings and his protection if we demand he leaves us alone?

I think it started when Madeleine Murray O'Hare complained she didn't want prayer in our schools and we said OK. Then someone said you'd better not read the Bible in school and we said OK. Then Dr Benjamin Spock said we shouldn't spank our children because their little personalities could be warped and we might damage their self-esteem and we said OK. Now we're asking why our children have no conscience, why they don't know right from wrong and why it doesn't bother them to kill strangers, their classmates and themselves.

Probably, if we think about it long enough, we can figure it out. I think it has a great deal to do with "We reap what we sow." Funny how simple it is for people to trash God and then wonder why the world's going to hell."

IS THE BIBLE WORTH MORE THAN ITS WEIGHT IN GOLD?

Here's a love letter from God. It's a compilation of quotations paraphrased from the Bible. It might help you to appreciate why God is so special and worthy of your interest. And why the Bible is so important.

"My Child

You may not know me but I know everything about you. I know when you sit down and when you rise up. I am familiar with all your ways. For you were made in my image. In me you live and move and have your being. For you are my offspring. I knew you even before you were conceived. I chose you when I planned creation. You were not a mistake, for all your days are written in my book. I determined the exact time of your birth and where you would live. You are fearfully and wonderfully made. I knit you together in your mother's womb. And brought you forth on the day you were born. I am not distant and angry but the complete expression of love.

It is my desire to lavish my love on you, simply because you are my child and I am your father. I offer you more than your earthly father ever could, for I am the perfect father. Every good gift you receive comes from my hand. I am your provider and I meet all your needs. My plan for your future has always been filled with hope because I love you with an everlasting love. I rejoice over you with singing. I will never stop doing good to you for you are my treasured possession.

If you seek me with all your heart you will find me. Delight in me and I will give you the desires of your heart. I am able to do more for you than you could possibly imagine. I am the Father who comforts you in all your troubles. When you are broken-hearted I am close to you.

I am your Father and I love you even as I love my son, Jesus. He came to demonstrate that I am for you not against you. Jesus died so that you and I could be reconciled. His death was the ultimate expression of my love for you. If you receive the gift of my son Jesus, you receive me. And nothing will ever separate you from my love again.

Almighty God"

Now, I can't imagine anyone wanting to tear up a letter like that, can you?

DON'T YOU DARE!

"One of the most powerful dramas of Christian faith ever written, this captivating allegory of man's religious journey in search of salvation follows the pilgrim as he travels an obstacle-filled road to the Celestial City. An enormously influential 17th century classic, universally known for its simplicity, vigour and beauty of language." Dover Publications.

What book is described here? It's sold over 10 million copies. In its day it sold more copies other than the Bible. Next to the Bible it has probably been more widely read than any other book in the English language. 15 years before his death, Gandhi wrote *"For the first time in fifty years I find myself in the Slough of Despond.."* It's in this book that the Slough of Despond is to be found.

The visitors' entrance to Christ Church College – Oxford has an inscription which reads *"My sword I give to him that shall succeed me in my pilgrimage."* These are the last words of Valiant-for-Truth before he crossed the River of Death as set out in this book.

On 31st October, 1847 the sailing vessel *John Williams* left Gravesend for the Pacific Islands. Its cargo included five thousand Bibles and four thousand copies of this book, in Tahitian.

When China's Communist government printed this book as an example of Western cultural heritage an initial printing of 200,000 copies sold out in three days.

"I marvel," said King Charles to Dr John Owen, *"that a learned man such as you can sit and listen to an unlearned tinker."* *"May it please your Majesty,"* replied he *"If I could possess the tinker's ability to grip men's hearts, I would gladly give in exchange all my learning."*

Tiya Soga was the first black South African to be ordained. His translation of this book into the Xhosa language has been called the most important literary influence in 19th century South Africa, after the Bible.

100,000 copies of this book were printed in English alone in 1692! Have you guessed? It's *Pilgrim's Progress*. A stained glass window is devoted to its author in Westminster Abbey. He was John Bunyan.

"It is wonderful that any man should have written a book of such universal and enduring popularity. More wonderful still that it should have been written in prison by an uneducated tinker, the descendant of a vagrant tribe – written spontaneously and unconsciously – not as an effort, but as a relief ...as the thoughts came crowding up in all their freshness." Robert Maguire D.D.

Don't you ever dare think that God can't use you.

JUST HOW NEAR IS THE KINGDOM OF GOD?

Can it be that the Kingdom of God is just a veil away? I mean we can't see God's kingdom, but it must be quite near us for every now and then we see something of what goes on there. So how do we know it's near us? Jesus told us so. Or rather he told the people of Galilee *"The Kingdom of God is near. Repent and believe the good news."*

Every now and then the veil seems to slip and we get a glimpse of what goes on. The angel visits the shepherds to announce the birth of Jesus. Whilst he is talking to them a heavenly host burst out of heaven. They can't hold back they are so excited. Then there's the occasion when Jesus is transfigured in front of some of his disciples. *"His clothes became dazzling white, whiter than anyone in the world could bleach them. And there appeared before them Elijah and Moses, who were talking with Jesus."* Then God speaks: *"This is my son, whom I love. Listen to him."*

That's pretty close. So what do these examples tell us if anything about that Kingdom? Two things. First, it's good news. We could do with some of that, couldn't we? Then, it's love. God loves Jesus who came to live and die amongst us because of God's love for us. Love is the key to the Kingdom – love God, love your neighbour.

But it's not just in the good times that the veil slips. Stephen was on trial for his life. He knew that his faith in Jesus as the Messiah was going to lead to his death. Indeed, his persecutors didn't even wait for a proper verdict. They dragged Stephen out of the city and stoned him to death. What a cruel way to die. So how near was he to the Kingdom of God? At the end of his defence he looked up to heaven and saw the glory of God, and Jesus. *"Look,"* he said, *"I see heaven open and the Son of Man standing at the right hand of God."* Near enough.

That was then; what about now? Have you ever laid hands of someone to pray for their healing and seen it happen in front of your eyes? Have you ever seen someone respond with joy and gladness to the good news? Then you will know that the Kingdom of God is near you. Why not enter and see for yourself how close you were?

EVERYTHING IN LIFE HAS CONSEQUENCES

Have you ever heard the expression "Body, mind and spirit"? It's those three elements that make us who we are. Our body enables us to do things – sitting, walking, crawling, standing, running, jumping, looking physically good. Our mind is just as important. It enables us to understand what makes our world the place it is, with its infinite variety of processes, how things work, what languages to speak, how to impress the opposite sex with your wit! We spend a lot of our day thinking – using our mind. But spirit? We all know what we mean by spirit. "He's high-spirited". "They've got wonderful team spirit". "That's a spirited horse." There's a spiritual element to us that's just as important as our body or mind.

The problem is that we have got things out of proportion. Huge industries have grown up that deal with our bodies one way or another – food, drink, sport, going to the gym, dieting, cosmetics, clothing, even hair transplants! And just think of the billions of pounds spent by the NHS to keep us in our bodies for as long as possible. Perhaps not so much compared to the body, but still quite a significant industry has grown up that deals with the mind. Walk into any library and look for the self-improvement shelves. Look in yellow pages for the number of practitioners who offer to help you straighten your minds out. See how many university students tack psychology onto their academic studies.

But when we come to spirit it's probably true to state that we don't really give it much thought. And that's really odd, because everything in life has consequences. If I don't look where I'm running I am liable to hurt myself (body). According to the experts, if I spend time watching pornography on the internet I am far more likely to commit a sexual offence in the future (mind). If my father broke my spirit when I was a youngster, I am far less likely to be able to take a proper role in society and my self-esteem will remain low (spirit).

If you think it's time you gave more attention to your spirit here's a good place to start. Jesus tells us that *"God is spirit and his worshippers must worship in spirit and truth."* A healthy spirit is one that has God at its centre. Why? Because God, who only wants the best for you, loves you and wants you to love him. That's a spiritual relationship. Try it. It has consequences.

DO YOU BELIEVE IN THE SUPERNATURAL?

Yes or No? Atheists don't. I don't see how they can believe in the supernatural and be proper atheists. In doing so they have put themselves in mortal danger, although they won't accept that. What they've done and are doing is mounting a very persuasive offensive to get people to agree with their rationale. In other words, making people into atheists by the power of their arguments. Turning them away from God. I wouldn't want that held against me on the Day of Judgment.

We have a very clear idea of the danger atheists are in when we look at the battle between David and Goliath in the Old Testament. We all know the story – David, a mere shepherd boy, defeats Goliath by slinging a stone at his forehead. But it's what he says before engaging Goliath that is relevant here. *"You come against me with sword and spear and javelin* (read "persuasive arguments and degrees") *but I come against you in the name of the Lord Almighty, the God of the armies of Israel, whom you have defied. This day the Lord will hand you over to me and I'll strike you down and cut off your head...and the whole world will know that there is a God in Israel....It is not by the sword or spear that the Lord saves, for the battle is the Lord's..."*

So Goliath dies. Since Jesus came things don't happen like that. Judgment will await our arrival before Jesus on our way to heaven or elsewhere. But, back to my question. Do you believe in the supernatural?

Do you believe in ghosts? Do you believe in life after death? Do you believe in astrology? Do you believe in fortune-tellers, in séances, in tarot cards, in witches and wizards, in strange things happening that can't be explained? A lot of people do. Well, if you believe in any of those, why don't you believe in Jesus? Everything he did that mattered was supernatural – healing people, calming the storm, turning water into wine, telling Peter what he was going to do before even Peter acknowledged it, foretelling his death and resurrection, coming back from the dead and rising to heaven. Even today, he can touch people's hearts and bring them to the foot of the cross, where he died for our sins, in repentance. It's all in the Bible.

Atheists have to eliminate the supernatural of the Bible, presumably by asserting that the story of Jesus is fiction. That's a lie.

THE REAL MEANING OF LIFE?

Mark 10:30
Revelation 21:4-8

Sometimes you have to laugh. Take the definition of a kiss. Imagine a young man on his first date. It's gone well. They've shared some laughs. There's genuine affection, some holding of hands and the expectation of further dates to come. On the doorstep the young man in saying goodbye says "May I touch or press your lips with my lips slightly pursed, then part them and emit a smacking sound in an expression of love, affection, greeting or reverence?" It's not going to work, is it? You wouldn't bother with the definition. You'd just get on with it.

But if I was a chum of yours, still waiting for a first kiss and asked you what it was like, you wouldn't use the definition either, would you? You'd say something like "It was wonderful. A sort of shock went through me. I felt so happy and alive. My heart started pounding. I wanted it never to stop". Well, you might not say it, being a cool dude, but you might feel it.

It's the same with life. You wouldn't go to a boring dictionary definition to extract the meaning of life. So when Jesus says *"I have come that they may have life and have it to the full"*, what's he talking about? We're all alive, aren't we?

It's necessary to go back into the area of romance. In the words of the song, love makes the world go round.

Don't you think a life without love is missing something, whether it's the love of a partner, family or friends? Love is an essential ingredient. Well, believe it or not, the love that Jesus offers you is better than any other kind. Why? First, because his love for you is so strong that he was prepared to die for you. Not many people would do that! Secondly, if you love him back, he will open the way to an eternal life with him.

Do we have any clues as to what eternal life might be like? John tells us. *"Now the dwelling of God is with men and he will live with them...He will wipe every tear from their eyes. There will be no more death or mourning or crying or pain."* And there won't be any of the following either : *"cowardly, unbelieving, vile, murderers, sexually immoral, those who practise magic arts, liars and those who worship other gods"*. Not a bad place to be. I'm looking forward to it. Join me?

WE'RE BRITISH; WE DON'T SHOW EMOTION

Whoever dreamt up the expression "stiff upper lip" deserves to be shot. I wonder how many relationships have disintegrated because one of the partners either didn't want to or couldn't show emotion.

The emotion I'm thinking about is joy. The church needs a healthy injection of the stuff. A church in Nice, France was celebrating its centenary. Their prayers included this *"Restore to us the joy of the resurrection."* That's what we need. However, the Bible doesn't help us much.

This is how it describes Jesus appearing to the disciples after his resurrection: *"The disciples were overjoyed when they saw the Lord."* That's it.

Imagine the scene from Peter's point of view. He must have been in torment, having disowned Jesus three times prior to Jesus' crucifixion. What a way to conclude a relationship – by deserting your companion, just after you've sworn to defend him with your life. Then Jesus appears to the disciples. How would Peter have re-acted to that? I think he would have hung back whilst the others greeted Jesus, distraught at his weakness.

Do you think Jesus would have left him in that state until they went fishing on Lake Galilee? I'm pretty sure Jesus would have called Peter to himself there and then and said something along the lines of "It's alright Peter. I knew you would deny me. I have forgiven you. Now come and join me in our celebrations. It's alright." Overjoyed probably doesn't do justice to Peter's response to Jesus.

The word "joy" is mentioned 244 times in the Bible. That's 87 more times than "heaven" and 190 times more than "hell". It's important. The apostles are flogged on the orders of the Sanhedrin. They "rejoiced" to have been counted worthy of suffering disgrace for the Name (Jesus). Phillip goes to a city in Samaria and heals many paralytics, cripples and those with mental diseases. As a result there was "great joy" in that city. Phillip then meets an important official in charge of all the treasury of Candace, queen of the Ethiopians. Phillip explains the gospel to him. He gets baptised and goes on his way "rejoicing".

Can you remember hearing the "Good news" and responding to it? This is what one priest wrote: "It's exhilarating to see people come to know Jesus Christ. I've seen people cry, beam with amazement, feel like a great weight has been lifted. The sky seems bluer, the grass greener and the future brighter" The sooner we bring back emotion the better.

WHO WANTS THE LIGHT OF LIFE?

Light is a wonderful thing. With it we can see the beauty of a rose, the majestic height of a mountain, the elegance of a surfer riding a wave, the smile on the face of a loved one, the green hills around us, the power and grace of an Olympic gymnast, the sinuous attacking crawl of a lion, even the flight of the bumblebee. Light is indeed a wonderful thing. Darkness, on the other hand, can provide us with none of those things. If it wasn't for the moon and the stars, night would be a most unsatisfactory business.

So, isn't it good that light can overcome darkness? One small torch can light up a room. One torch on the front of a bicycle can light up the path to be taken. How welcoming is the front porch light to the office worker walking home from the station.

John appreciated the difference. He was the disciple that Jesus loved and there is no doubting his love for Jesus.

So what words did he use to describe Jesus' arrival on earth when he came to write the beginning of his Gospel? He used the comparison of light and darkness.

He had had decades to think about his time with Jesus. This, in some of the most majestic words and phrases you are ever likely to read, is what he wrote:

"In the beginning was the word and the word was with God and the word was God. He was with God in the beginning. Through him all things were made; without him nothing was made that has been made. In him was life and that life was the light of men. The light shines in the darkness, but the darkness has not understood it."

Here's an explanation. Jesus is God in human form. He had to adopt human form in order that we would be able to see him and relate to him. God needed him to come to earth to rescue us from a life lived in darkness. Yes, without God we live in darkness. Jesus showed us the way back to God. Those of us who accept that way are brought into the light; those who do not continue to live in darkness with all the awful consequences that result.

Jesus himself said *"I am the light of the world. Whoever follows me will never walk in darkness, but will have the light of life."*

For pity's sake, come out of the darkness. Follow Jesus and he'll bring you into the light of life.

WHY SHOULD ANYONE LOVE YOU?

Psalm 33:13-15
John 3:16

A recent newspaper article stated that marriages tend to last longer than "partnerships". It also noted that divorces are rising. So, there are a lot of marriage style relationships that don't last. Do you think a major reason for such separations might be that it's only after a relationship starts that one partner finds out what the other partner is really like?

I have a proposal to solve this problem. I could develop an internet programme containing a description of everything the person you're thinking about allying yourself to has ever done wrong. For instance, you are thinking of starting a relationship with John. You look him up on the internet . You find that John has been caught driving under the influence on many occasions. He also fiddles his expense account at his work and is about to get the sack. He had a relationship with Julie but that ended when he punched her and broke her arm. You might think twice about starting a relationship with John. Such a programme would be really useful and I could be a mega-millionaire in no time. Facebook would love to buy me out.

But there's a problem with this suggestion. If everyone could find out about all your bad characteristics, why would anyone ever want to start a life-long relationship with you - or anyone else, come to that? Life as we know it would come to an end and I would be responsible.

So I'm not going to do it. But suppose there was someone who did know everything about you, including all your faults, and still wanted to have a life-long relationship with you. It seems to me that person would be a fool, crazy or someone extraordinarily special.

Well, there is someone who wants to have that relationship and he's not a fool or crazy. Let me introduce you to God. He knows all about you. Listen to this: *"From heaven the Lord looks down and sees all mankind, from his dwelling place he watches all who live on earth – he who forms the hearts of all, who considers everything they do."*

God knows everything about us and he still loves us. How do we know? Jesus told us: *"For God so loved the world* (that's you and me) *that he gave his one and only son that whosoever believed in him should not perish but have everlasting life."* That's a life-long relationship with God through Jesus. Interested? Worth thinking about?

WITH WHOM WILL YOU BE SEEKING AN ALLIANCE?

In the fifth century BC Thucydides wrote a history of the Peloponnesian Wars, providing a detailed contemporary account of the life-and-death struggle between two giants of Greek history – Athens and Sparta. Thucydides was Athenian. He achieved the rank of general in the earlier stages of the war. "He applied a passion for accuracy and a contempt for myth and romance in

compiling his factual record of a disastrous conflict."
That's the blurb on a Penguin Classics book called
"Thucydides: The Peloponnesian War."

On the basis of such a resounding reference as to
accuracy, we can approach the history itself with
reasonable confidence that what's written actually
happened. And we are not alone in this confidence.
Historians and academics are similarly confident. So,
let's review one aspect of the build up to this war.

Athens and Sparta had built up alliances with other
Greek city states. One city state outside these alliances,
Corcyra, was in dispute with Corinth. Worried at the
build up of the Corinthian navy, the Corcyrans visit
Athens to seek an alliance. Thanks to Thucydides we can
repeat what the Corcyran representative said when he
addressed the Athenian assembly. Here's an extract
spoken 2,400 years ago:

*"Athenians, in a situation like this, it is right and proper
that first of all certain points should be made clear. We
have come to ask you for help, but cannot claim that this
help is due to us because of any great services we have
done to you in the past or on the basis of any existing
alliance. We must therefore convince you first that
by giving us this help you will be acting in your own
interests, or certainly not against your own interests;
and then we must show that our gratitude can be
depended upon. If on all these points you find our
arguments unconvincing, we must not be surprised if
our mission ends in failure."*

So when, four hundred years or so later we find a "detailed contemporary account" of Jesus' ministry, set out in the Bible, are we wrong to assert that a similar "passion for accuracy and contempt for myth and romance" was present in its compilation?

Thucydides history was of a life-and-death struggle between Athens and Sparta. The Bible provides us with a history of a life-and-death struggle between good and evil. Athenians and Spartans were fighting and dying for territorial domination. Jesus was fighting and dying for your soul. With whom will you be seeking an alliance?

SIN, SINNER, SINNEST

Sadly, the Bible isn't all fun and games. Not by a long shot. How do you like this sentence, for example: *"There is no-one righteous; not even one."* ? Don't you take offence at that? Don't you think "Well, I think I'm a good person. I do my best and try hard. You can't do better than that." But it's not "goodness" the Bible is talking about, it's "righteousness". We just don't measure up. How can we when Jesus raises the bar so high that no-one can rise to it. Listen to this: *"You have heard it said "Love your neighbour and hate your enemy". But I tell you: "Love your enemies and pray for those who persecute you."* I bet you don't all do that. He also said that if you break one law you've broken the lot. So, not loving your enemies or praying for those who persecute you means you're a law-breaker. Do you know what that makes you? The answer is in the Bible. If you're not righteous you're a sinner.

Now, if there is one word in the English language that lays claim to being the most unpopular it has to be "sinner". No-one likes being accused of being a "sinner". In fact, we avoid using that word at all if we possibly can. I don't suppose there are many young people today who are aware of the implications of that word. Yet, as we've already seen, the Bible makes it clear that we are all sinners and the wages of sin are death.

One of the ten commandments is to honour your mother and father. Not phone them once a week to make sure they're still alive. Not invite them over for lunch once a quarter. Not hate them for trying to apply some rules and order to your life as a teenager. It means giving them priority, showing you really care, showing respect, being obedient to their (reasonable) wishes. If you knew that not obeying that commandment would keep you out of heaven you'd take it seriously, wouldn't you?

If sin is death, where's life? Jesus was sent by God proclaiming that he was "the way, the truth and the life". Jesus knew we couldn't match up to the standards of a God who is holy and demands holiness from us. Jesus died to cancel out our sins, make us holy and thus open our way to heaven. Life without Jesus ends with death and hell. With him eternal life and heaven await. Ready?

IS THIS THE GREATEST LOVE STORY EVER TOLD?

In spite of what the Bible tells us, much of why God does what He does is a mystery to us. That may not be such a bad thing. Possibly a reason why so many of us love and support the Queen is that we don't know everything about her.

Why did God create us in the first place? I mean, right from the start we have done our best to ruin our world and our relationships with God and each other The Bible tells us: *"The Lord saw how great man's wickedness on earth had become....and was grieved that he had made man...and his heart was filled with pain."* So we had the flood that wiped everything out to enable God to start again with Noah.

Then God tells Abraham:*"I will make you into a great nation* (Israel) *and I will bless you...all peoples on earth will be blessed through you."* As we read on in the Old Testament we find that if all nations are to be blessed through Israel then Israel must adhere to a set of rules and regulations, including the well-known ten commandments. The penalty for failing to adhere to these regulations is exile and, instead of blessing all nations, being scattered amongst them. That's just what happened.

For some reason God doesn't give up on us. He can't destroy us, even though we are behaving as badly as mankind did before God destroyed them in the flood. Why? Because God made a covenant not to. So we come to God's latest throw. I can't begin to imagine the conversation that takes place between God and Jesus. What I can tell you is that it must have included the mission that Jesus, the son of God, would placate God by taking on himself the guilt for everything that we have done, are doing and will do wrong. In other words, Jesus would die for our sins, instead of us.

In a nutshell, God loves us so much that He is prepared to see his only son die in our place. Isn't that love of the highest order?

So what's our role in all of this? Doesn't it look as though we are off the hook without having to do anything? Well, there is one thing that we have to do – believe that Jesus was who he said he was – the Son of God – then live our lives in a way that pleases him. Not a bad price to pay, is it?

ARE OUR FEET IN GOOD SHAPE?

When did you last take a good look at your feet? I mean a really close look? I looked at mine the other day. They're not very attractive! I put it down to two years of stamping around parade grounds at Sandhurst, yomping at high speed for long distances over broken ground, parachuting, racing over three miles, cross-country running and rugby. I expect most men have similar stories, particularly those who played football. But, just think how much worse they might have been if I had had to do all that without wearing any shoes. I suppose you might think that my feet might have been healthier but, somehow, I doubt it.

So take yourself back to Israel two thousand years ago. It was very unlikely that children living out in the country had anything to wear on their feet. And I should think that applied to a lot of grown-ups as well. It was dusty and dirty and when the wind blew the sand and dust would cling to the legs of anyone having to travel.

One of the most menial jobs of any household of that day would be to untie the sandals of the visitors and wash their feet. Can you imagine in what state those feet must have been if the traveller had walked to the house, even if he'd been wearing sandals? So when John the Baptist is looking for a metaphor to describe his relationship to Jesus he cannot think of anything more demeaning of himself than to say *"He is the one who comes after me the thongs of whose sandals I am not worthy to untie."*

One of the last things Jesus did before the events leading up to his crucifixion was to wash his disciples' feet. It wasn't a symbolic act. It was a dirty, menial thing to do. It was his way of demonstrating what being a servant to each other meant. *"Do you understand what I have done for you?...Now that I, your Lord and teacher, have washed your feet you also should wash one another's feet.*

Nowadays we have the ceremony whereby the Archbishop of Canterbury washes the feet of those attending the appropriate service. Whilst that is a symbolic act, it nonetheless establishes a determination to take seriously Jesus' command to be servants to each other.

We therefore have a challenge to face up to. Do our church members take seriously that command? Are we servants to each other? Are our feet in good shape?

WOULD YOU LIKE TO MEET AN ANGEL?

The Bible is littered with angels. They were quite active during the period after Israel had established itself in Canaan. An angel visited Gideon. Israel had got itself into a mess thanks to not holding faithfully to God. As a result nations around Israel were attacking and inflicting grievous hardship. So the angel tells Gideon that God is going to use him to rescue Israel. On that occasion the angel came as a messenger.

There are other occasions when an angel is put to work. One is when King David decides to hold a census of the fighting men in Israel and Judah. This displeased God because David was looking to the strength of his own fighting men rather than relying on God. So God gives David a choice of punishment – three years of famine, three months of fleeing from enemies or three days of plague. David chooses to fall into the hands of God rather than men, so God sends an angel to inflict three days of plague.

On another occasion Israel was again in sore distress. The Assyrians had invaded the land and were besieging Jerusalem. An angel of the lord goes out and destroys 185,000 Assyrians overnight. The occasion is immortalised in one of Lord Byron's most famous poems which starts majestically:

> *"The Assyrian came down like the wolf on the fold*
> *And his cohorts were gleaming in purple and gold;"*

Around the time Jesus was born angels were pretty active. An angel visited Zechariah in the Temple to tell him about the birth of John the Baptist. Then an angel visited Mary to tell her about the forthcoming birth of her son, son of God. Then an angel visited the shepherds to tell them where to find the baby Jesus. God used angels as messengers to deliver some of the most important information we are ever likely to receive.

Jesus refers to angels as well. When Jesus is about to be arrested prior to his crucifixion one of his followers tries to defend him with his sword. Jesus observes that his Father would at once put more than twelve legions of angels at his disposal if he wished. However, Jesus goes on to say *"how then would the Scriptures be fulfilled...?"* There were roughly 6,000 soldiers in a legion. So Jesus was talking about more than 72,000 angels. Jesus chose to go to the cross to save us rather call on angels to save himself. They're out there alright. Would you like to meet one?

WHAT MAKES YOU THINK THE GOSPELS ARE TRUE?

Son: Dad, why do you think the Gospels are true and not made up?
D: Figs, temples, prophecy, and dates.
S: What?
D: There's a curious little story in Matthew's Gospel about a fig tree. Jesus is on his way back from the temple. It's early morning. He's hungry and goes to pick a fig.

However, there are none on the tree so he says *"May you never bear fruit again."* The tree immediately withers. Why is this story even in Matthew's Gospel? I think it's because Matthew wanted to show that every word Jesus uttered, however insignificant, was true. And that makes sense. If you want people to believe that Jesus is special you'll want to show how that works out, even in the smallest detail.

Now, imagine a temple 150 feet high, 90 feet wide and as long standing on a hill, clad in gold which could be seen shining from miles away. How impressive for those days! It certainly impressed Jesus' disciples. Yet Jesus prophesies of the temple that *"not one stone will be left on another. They will all be thrown down."* And so it came to pass. In AD66, Jerusalem revolted against the Romans. Titus, the Roman commander, came with four legions besieged, captured and, in AD70, destroyed the city and its temple leaving not one stone on another, just as Jesus had prophesied. Over 1.1million Jews died during the siege. It was just about the worst thing of many that happened to Jerusalem in centuries. It was massive and appalling.

Now, don't you think that if the Gospels include a story about something as insignificant as a fig tree they would be bound to include the coming to pass of Jesus' extraordinary prophecy about the destruction of the temple that had such a terrible impact on Israel? But they don't. Not a word.

For this reason at least one school of thought, to which I belong, believes the Gospels must have been written before AD70. I mean how do you record Jesus as a prophet at the least and then ignore his second most important prophecy of all? And another thing: a lot of people would have still been alive when the Gospels were written who would have known about Jesus and been able to say if the Gospels were a load of cobblers. They didn't. Instead, followers of Jesus spread like wildfire throughout the Roman Empire. That's why I think the Gospels are true.

S: Thanks Dad, but what's Jesus most important prophecy?

WOULD YOU DIE FOR A MYTH?

The first case of imperial persecution of Christians took place in Rome under Nero In 64AD when a great fire broke out, destroying parts of the city and economically damaging the population. Suetonius, a Roman historian, suspected Nero himself was the arsonist stating that, *"Nero fastened the guilt and inflicted the most exquisite tortures on a class hated for their abominations, called Christians..."* That, incidentally, gives you some idea how fast Christianity spread from the time of Jesus' crucifixion in 33AD to 64AD when there were enough of them in Rome to take such blame. Some early Christians sought out and welcomed martyrdom. In 185, the proconsul of Asia (then part of Turkey) was approached by a group of Christians demanding to be executed. He obliged some of them but told the others that there was plenty of rope available or cliffs that they could jump off. There are many documented examples of martyrdom from history.

Persecution of Christians has carried on down through the centuries to the present day. In 614AD, according to early Christian chroniclers, 26,000 Jewish rebels entered Jerusalem as part of a Persian army and massacred any Christians found there. Some 60,000 Christians died in the massacre. The Jews offered to help them escape death if they became Jews and denied Christ. This they refused to do.

By 1630, some 300,000 Japanese Christians had been suppressed and driven underground. According to Pope Benedict XVI, Christians are the most persecuted group in the world. According to the World Evangelical Alliance over 200 million Christians in at least 60 countries are denied fundamental human rights solely because of their faith.

Now I think you have to ask yourselves "Were or are they all ignorant, stupid or mad even?" What on earth gave them the determination to suffer cruel torture for their faith, even unto death? Could it have been a myth? Or a nice story? A wonderful bedtime book that helped you to sleep well when the light got turned out? Why didn't they just say *"OK, I am not going to die if that's what happens to you when you become a Christian, so I'll renounce my faith?"* Or could it be that they believed what they read in the Bible, heard from their leaders, experienced in their own lives or saw in the lives of fellow Christians around them? You decide.

WHERE'S THE PERSECUTION?

Jesus' persecution culminated in his death. The Book of Acts tells us quite a lot about the persecutions that then followed. It tells us that Stephen was the first martyr and that persecutions broke out against the early church. The Book of Acts ends with the story of Paul's trials and persecution. In a romantic sense you could say that the early church was founded on the blood of the martyrs.

As faith in Jesus spread it was seen as a threat to the Roman Empire, particularly once the emperors began regarding themselves as living gods who could stand no competition. So persecutions then followed with the full backing of the might of the Roman Empire. The first of these was under the Emperor Nero in the second half of the first century but further persecutions followed under Domitian, Trajan, Marcus Aurelius, Decius, Valerian, Diocletian and Julian, right up to AD315 when Constantine became emperor. Some estimates put the number of martyred Christians as high as 100,000. Yet this didn't stop the church growing at a phenomenal rate.

Today, physical persecution of Christians occurs in many countries. China is an interesting case in point. The Communist Party, that runs China, is violently opposed to any threat to its hegemony. Many Christians have suffered death or imprisonment at its hands. The extraordinary thing is that this has had little impact on the growth of Christianity in China. In fact, it was estimated recently that China will soon become the nation with the largest number of Christians anywhere on earth. One Chinese leader, imprisoned for 17 years, was released to discover that in his absence his church had grown from hundreds to hundreds of thousands. Estimates of the number of Christians in China are in the order of 150 million although, for obvious reasons, it's not possible to make a fully accurate assessment.

This leads one to wonder whether one of the reasons the church in the West is in decline may be that it is not being persecuted. Or could it be that there is persecution but of a different type – and we are ducking it? Could it be that we have been assimilated into our society and no longer stand out from the rest of the population? And don't want to? Is it that we don't bring Jesus into our normal everyday life because we don't want to be mocked, scorned or insulted or upset anyone? Are we serving Jesus in our way rather than his? I wonder what the early Christians would think about that.

WHERE ARE THE PROPHETS?

In Old Testament times, around 900-800BC, God spoke directly to individuals or indirectly through prophets like Samuel and Nathan. His message was pretty clear and usually something to do with keeping his laws and getting blessed or worshipping other gods and getting zapped.

On a previous occasion we read how Solomon was faced with such a choice and got it wrong. Why was this? Well, in Solomon's case, it was either politics or testosterone. I mean, why did he need 700 wives, many from other countries, and 300 concubines? It's absurd. It got him into a tragic muddle and he lost sight of the God who had given him everything in the first place.

You have to hand it to the authors of the Old Testament. They tell the story warts and all. No fudging of the history of Israel, quite unlike some countries – China? Russia? It's one reason why the Old Testament can be trusted.

But, getting back to God's message, you can see how things go pear-shaped for Israel. After Solomon's reign there are now two states – Judah and Israel. Israel has broken away from Judah and appointed Jeroboam as its king. Now Jeroboam is a clever chap. He's worked out that there won't be real separation from Judah unless he can stop Israelites from worshipping at the temple in Jerusalem. So he says to the people of Israel *"It is too much for you to go up to Jerusalem. Here are your gods…"*

Now, at the time of the exodus from Egypt, about 550 years previously, Israel got into bad trouble with God. This was because Moses, their leader, had disappeared up Mount Sinai and they thought they'd lost him for good. So they made a golden calf to worship - a move that ended badly. So now we have Jeroboam providing gods for Israel to worship – and what are they? You've guessed it, golden calves, two of them. Worse, anyone who wanted to could become a priest, although God had chosen the tribe of Levi to be his priestly tribe. The result was total disaster. God wiped Jeroboam and his house from the face of the earth.

So have we, today, any reason to suppose that we can worship anything or anyone we like and ignore God? Worship our bodies? Worship our finances? Worship our cars or property? Worship footballers or pop idols? Where are the prophets to warn us of the disaster that awaits if we live without regard for God? In the Bible?

THERE'S A REAL FIGHT GOING ON

"For our struggle is not against flesh and blood but against the rulers, against the authorities, against the powers of this dark world and against the spiritual forces of evil in the heavenly realms" Ephesians 6:12

If you have spent your day fighting off the temptations of this world and return home satisfied you have won, you are to be congratulated but you are merely skirmishing; you are not fighting in the main battle - against the powers of this dark world. That's where the real fight is. So what are these powers?

Jesus goes into the wilderness and spends forty days there. Whilst he's there Satan comes to tempt him, probably in a spiritual way. Now, here's a question. Who is the ruler of this dark world? It's got to be Satan. Why? Well, who else can offer Jesus all the authority and splendour of all the kingdoms of the world– and mean it – if he didn't have that authority and splendour to give in the first place? Thank God, Jesus turns him down. But when Jesus talks about setting people free he means from the power of Satan and the dark world he controls. The fight is on.

This is how it works. As John wrote in his Gospel *"In him (Jesus) was life and that life was the light of men. The light shines in the darkness , but the darkness has not understood it."* Those were John's words but they agree with what Jesus said of himself *"I am the light of the world...whoever follows me...will have the light of life."* In other words, if you are a follower of Jesus you are the light of Jesus, shining in this dark world. Keep that thought in mind.

Jesus had some pithy words to say about light *"You are the light of the world. A city on a hill cannot be hidden. Neither do people light a lamp and put it under a bowl. Instead they put it on its stand and it gives light to everyone in the house. In the same way, let your light shine before men, so that they may see your good deeds and praise your Father in heaven."*

Darkness cannot exist in the presence of light, can it? So, is there an easy way to start bringing light into the darkness, to fight the spiritual fight? Yes, there is. We call it praying. Pray peace and blessings on your friends and neighbours every day. You love them, don't you?

WHAT ME? SUPERSTITIOUS? AM I REALLY?

Well, let's find out. According to Collins Concise Dictionary – it's only 1,657 pages long – one of the definitions of superstition is *"any irrational belief especially with regard to the unknown"*.

Here are some examples of this "irrational belief" with which you are almost certainly familiar

- Friday the thirteenth is an unlucky day
- A rabbit's foot brings good luck
- To find a four leaf clover is good luck
- To walk under a ladder brings bad luck
- To break a mirror brings seven years bad luck
- To open an umbrella in the house brings bad luck
- An itchy palm means money will come your way
- Touch wood!

I expect you know lots more of these but please don't send them to me!

Now the way I see it, anyone who is superstitious is consciously or unconsciously accepting that there is some greater power, unknown to them, who will exercise its ability to dispense good or bad luck depending on what event has taken place - a sort of cosmic hero who has focused on you because you conformed to some superstitious regulation. Of course, in the case of Friday the thirteenth everyone in the whole world is under that focus, as it's an unlucky day for us all. Our unknown cosmic hero is going to be remarkably busy making sure everyone has their fair share of bad luck on that day.

We Christians have a cosmic hero too. We call him God. One of the main differences between our cosmic hero and the cosmic hero of the superstitious is that we know who our hero is. And we know what he's like. How do we know? Well, Jesus covered this in discussion with one of his disciples. Philip says to Jesus *"Lord, show us the Father (i.e. God) and that will be enough for us."* Jesus gets quite indignant at this point. *"Don't you know me,*

Philip, even after I have been among you for such a long time? Anyone who has seen me has seen the Father."

Fine, so what can Jesus tell us about the Father? Well, he goes on in his conversation with Philip *"....at least believe on the evidence of the miracles themselves."* So, the miracles Jesus performed give you some idea of what God is like. What were those miracles? Some examples: healing the sick, opening the eyes of the blind, curing leprosy and epilepsy, raising the dead to life.

I know which cosmic hero I prefer. What about you?

CAN YOU SAY "IT IS WELL WITH MY SOUL"?

Horatio G Spafford was a prominent Chicago lawyer of the 1860's. He was rich and successful. He had everything going for him. But he suffered almost unimaginable personal tragedy. In 1870 his son was killed by scarlet fever at the age of four. A year later it was fire rather than fever that struck. Horatio had invested heavily in real estate on the shores of Lake Michigan. In 1871, every one of those holdings was wiped out by the great Chicago fire.

Horatio decided to take his wife and four daughters on a holiday to England, partly to help recover from these tragedies and partly to help DL Moody. Moody was a great evangelist of that time. He was travelling around Britain on one of his campaigns. Horatio and his wife, Anna, planned to join him in 1873.

And so the six of them travelled to New York in November of that year, from where they were to catch the French steamer "Ville de Havre". However, just before they set sail, a last minute business development forced Horatio to delay. Not wanting to ruin the family holiday, Horatio persuaded his family to go as planned and he would follow later. Just nine days later Horatio received a telegram. It was from Anna in Wales. It read: "Saved alone."

On November 22nd, 1873 the "Ville de Havre" collided with "The Lochearn", an English vessel. It sank in only 12 minutes, claiming the lives of 226 people. Anna stood on the deck, with her daughters Annie, Maggie, Bessie and Tanetta clinging desperately to her. Her last memory was of her baby being torn violently from her arms by the force of the waves. Anna was only saved from drowning by a plank which floated beneath her unconscious body and propped her up.

Upon hearing this terrible news, Horatio boarded the next ship out of New York to join his bereaved wife. During the voyage the captain called Horatio to the bridge. "A careful reckoning has been made." he said, "and I believe we are now passing the place where the "Ville de Havre" was wrecked." Horatio then returned to his cabin and penned the lyrics of his great hymn. It starts:

> "When peace like a river attendeth my way
> When sorrow like sea billows roll.
> Whatever my lot, Thou has taught me to say
> It is well, it is well with my soul."

Can you say "It is well with my soul"?

SO WHERE'S GOD THEN?

King Solomon knew where he was. So did two million Israelites. Two million? King David had a census taken. It established there were 800,000 men who could handle a sword living in Israel and 500,000 such men living in Judah. Add in all the others because they were too young, too old or disabled or women and two million seems a conservative figure

Anyway, how did King Solomon and the two million know where God was? Because Solomon built a temple for him. It was 90 feet long, 30 feet wide and 45 feet tall. It took seven years to build. He used 80,000 stonecutters, 70,000 carriers and 3,300 foremen. Then God told Solomon *"I have consecrated this temple by putting my Name there, for ever. My eyes and my heart will always be there."* God was going to live amongst the nation he had chosen for himself. As always, there was a sting in the tail because Israel had to obey God's laws and not serve other gods. If that happened God would reject the temple. Well, we all know what happened, sadly.

So if God's not there then where is he?

Paul, that extraordinary Christian evangelist of the first century, knew where he wasn't. Paul is on one of his missionary journeys. It has taken him to Athens. He does what he always does which was to choose somewhere significant and start talking about Jesus. The Athenians, who loved to debate, invited Paul to speak to the Council of the Areopagus. This is what he said: *"The God who made the world and everything in it is the Lord of heaven and earth and does not live in temples built by hands."*

At this point Paul would almost certainly have lifted his arm and pointed to the now world-famous Parthenon temple sitting atop the Acropolis. It was impressive – 202 feet long by 101 feet wide. Its marbles, on display at the British Museum, give only a limited idea of its impressive standing. How proud the Athenians must have been of it and how shocked to hear that Athena, the goddess worshipped there, was inferior to Paul's God. No doubt the members of the Areopagus were interested to know where Paul's God was. So Paul tells them that God wants us to reach out for him and find him, though he is not far from each one of us. *"For in him we live and move and have our being."*

So where's God then? With us, around us, within us. Enjoy.

WOULD YOU LIKE TO BE PART OF A TEMPLE?

That's an odd question, don't you think? I mean a temple in Christian circles, usually means either Solomon's temple, referred to in the Old Testament, or Herod's temple, referred to in the New Testament,.

Imagine for a moment what those temples would have been like. At least three words spring to mind – crowded, noisy, bloody. First, it was a requirement of the law that all Israelites worshipped at the temple. At the height of its power Israel's population must have run to over 2 million. Just 1% worshipping at any one time meant 20,000 on site. Crowded and noisy! What about the blood? Well, the priests were there to make sacrifices on behalf of the people. To give just one example, when King Solomon dedicated the temple on its completion there were sacrificed 22, 000 cattle and 120,000 sheep and goats. Blood everywhere! It would have been noisy as well because, by Jesus' time, many teachers of the law would gather followers around them and teach in the temple area, with discussion and question and answer. In the temple was found the pinnacle of the law and regulations.

But there is another sort of temple. Paul writes about it in his hard-hitting letter to the Ephesians. First of all, however, you've got to get past this: *"As for you, you were dead in your transgressions and sins in which you used to live when you followed ways of this world."* That's not very nice, is it? You Ephesians were dead, he writes! As he's writing to the Ephesians, we might feel he wasn't referring to us. Don't you believe it! He goes on *"All of us lived amongst them (the world) at one time."* No escape there. Fortunately, Paul knows that God has thrown us a lifeline. *"Because of his great love for us, God...made us alive with Christ even when we were dead in transgressions."*

So what's this got to do with temples? Well, this is how Paul describes who and what we are now. *"You are fellow-citizens with God's people and members of God's household, built on the foundation of the apostles and prophets, with Christ Jesus himself as the chief cornerstone. In him the whole building is joined together to become a holy temple in the Lord... in which God lives by his Sprit."*

Would you like to be made alive in Christ, with God living in you by his Spirit? Would you like to be part of that temple?

PLEASE TELL ME WHAT HAPPENED

Luke 13

Pastor: "I've called this extraordinary meeting of the Ministry Team because I want to know what happened last Sunday. So will someone please tell me?"

Assistant Pastor: "Yes, I will. We had a group of visitors, about 13 or 14 of them. I didn't like the look of them right from the beginning. First of all, they sat anywhere they wanted. Several of us weren't able to sit where we usually do. Major Cousens insisted on sitting in his usual place so they all cramped up to get him in. He wasn't at all comfortable and got very cross. Then they started praising God and raising their hands in worship – quite inappropriate as the service hadn't even started. I went up to the man who seemed to be their leader and asked him to tell them to be quiet. Do you know what he said?"

P "Of course I don't; I wasn't there!"

AP: "He said "I tell you, if they keep quiet the stones will cry out." Now what sort of answer was that? Anyway, at that moment the choir came in and they quietened down while we sang the first hymn. Then, you won't believe what happened next. Old Mrs Jamieson came in.

You know, the one with the spinal defect that leaves her bent over? One of the strangers saw her, got up and went to her side and helped her to take his seat."

P: "Well, what's wrong with that?"

AP: "Instead of sitting down this stranger goes up the front and, to our amazement, delivers the sermon. That put the scheduled preacher's nose out of joint! But it gets worse. In the middle of his sermon he calls Mrs Jamieson out. She hobbles to the front and this is what he said: *"Woman, you are set free from your infirmity."* Then he put his hands on her, and immediately she straightened up and praised God."

P: "What? Right in the middle of the service? What did you do about it?"

AP: " As soon as they both sat down, I went up to the front and tried to restore order. What I said was something along the lines of "Look everyone, we have prayer for healing after the service, so please let's behave in a decent and orderly manner and finish our service without any more interruptions." That's when the strangers left, muttering something about hypocrites. The congregation started cheering them which left me totally humiliated. You've got to do something!

BE AFRAID; BE VERY AFRAID!

If I was thinking of becoming an atheist, wouldn't it make sense for me to check out both sides of the argument? I ought to know what I am dismissing if I decide that there is no God. So, I guess the first place I would start would be the Bible – not the Old Testament, the New Testament.

There, I would come across not only Jesus but also the people who journeyed with him for three years across the hills and valleys, villages, towns and cities of Israel – the apostles Peter and Matthew, both of whom wrote Gospels. Then there is Mark, who was Peter's disciple and, of course, Paul whose conversion to Christianity is one of the most dramatic recorded. Paul met with the apostles. His subsequent writings, recorded in the New Testament, bear witness to that.

Then, I would have to decide whether the four Gospels are a myth. It's true that there are differences between the Gospels but none that contradict the fact of Jesus' miracles, teaching, crucifixion and resurrection – surely the most significant aspects of his story. As the police know only too well, the descriptions given by four witnesses to an accident will not necessarily coincide on all details. They will, however, confirm that an accident took place.

If I could pick just one part of the New Testament to look at closely, it wouldn't be a Gospel, at least not to start with. It would be the second of Peter's two letters recorded there. There's one passage in Chapter 2 of that letter that I would make compulsory reading for anyone who's thinking about atheism. It's verses 4 to 10. This is what they say:

"For if God did not spare angels when they sinned, but sent them to hell, putting them into gloomy dungeons to be held for judgment; if he did not spare the ancient world when he brought the flood on its ungodly people….; if he condemned Sodom and Gomorrah by

burning them to ashes as an example of what is going to happen to the ungodly; if this is so, then the Lord knows how to rescue godly men from trials and to hold the unrighteous for the day of judgment. This is especially true of those who follow the corrupt desire of the sinful nature and despise authority."

God is not a helpless babe in a Christmas manger. But, if you do decide against him, be very clear of what awaits when you make the wrong call.

HOW DO YOU KNOW?

Son: "Dad. Can I ask you a question?"

Dad: "Sure."

Son: "Well, you've written all these articles for the Parish Magazine. So it looks like you know a lot about what's in the Bible. But have you any personal experiences? Like how the Holy Spirit impacts your life? Otherwise it's all impersonal and you're just quoting what others have said or opinion."

Dad: "As it happens I have many personal experiences but I'll just stick to one. It happened about a year or so after I committed my life to Jesus. What you need to know is that there was a time when I was an insecure sort of person. For instance, believe it or not, speaking in public was a huge strain for me. Being a lawyer meant I had to do that quite often. I was so worried about it I used to learn all my speeches by heart.

The day came when for the first time I had to give a presentation to the Board of Directors of the company

I worked for. Now these were men who had reached the pinnacle of success. The great and the good from all walks of life in the City. They were tough, no nonsense sort of people. I don't mind telling you I was overwhelmed. I learned what I was going to say and I was happy with that. But when the day arrived and I was waiting outside the Board Room I was in a real panic. I just knew I couldn't deliver. It was going to be a disaster. To make matters worse, the person who presented before me came out looking very shaken.

So I did the sensible thing and cried out to God to help me. I hated having to battle my nerves every time I opened my mouth in public. I wanted it to stop. What I said was "God, you have got to help me. I can't do this by myself." Almost immediately a most extraordinary thing happened. It was as though I had stepped into a warm shower. I felt a heat that started at my head and slowly made its way down my body. My whole body warmed up. I don't know how long the sensation lasted, probably not more than a couple of minutes. But when it left me I was totally confident of what I had to do and sailed through my presentation. And I haven't stopped talking since!"

Son: "I can vouch for that!"

ALWAYS BE READY

If you travel with God you had better be ready because He will provide opportunities for you to share your faith.

I was travelling from Washington DC to London Heathrow. I can't tell you how pleased I was to be upgraded to first class. As I settled myself into my seat I wondered who would be my travelling companion – a politician, a financier, perhaps a film star or a pop idol. What I got was a very ordinary looking sort of person. As he lowered himself into his seat he introduced himself. After that, the first thing he said was "I'm paying my own way. I'm taking a week out. I've got one or two issues to resolve."

I had a sinking feeling that he was going to share these issues with me. Sure enough, over supper, he launched into his story. It appeared that he had had a childhood sweetheart. Sadly they had lost touch with each other when she and her family moved away. He had then joined the US Navy and got posted to Pearl Harbour. When he retired from the Navy he qualified as an accountant, got married and had a family. One day a friend of his told him he had met his childhood sweetheart and had her telephone number. Would he like it?

The answer was "Yes". A phone call later and contact had been re-established. They had met up again and were now enjoying a resumption of the passion that had coloured their relationship all those years ago. So, here they were. Both married with families, deciding whether to leave them and start life anew together. They were taking a week away from each other to have a good think and come to their respective decisions.

The story took most of supper to tell. He then looked at me and asked "What do you think?" I told him I only had one thing to say. "God hates adultery." I went on "But don't take my word for it. You can borrow a book of Psalms and Proverbs from the Bible given to me by Billy Graham. You've got a week so you should be able to read your way through it and find some guidance." I left my business card in the book so he could return it.

About three weeks later the book turned up in my office. In it was a blank card on which was written "Thanks. It helped me reach the right decision." Always be ready.

WHY SHOULD I BECOME A CHRISTIAN?

Ed: "You know, Nick, there's something I've been meaning to ask you for some time. You're always going on about how being a Christian is so great. Alright, not always but you've certainly mentioned it a few times. But you've never really explained to me why it's so great. I mean, look at my family. My dad's a bigwig in the city, earning a fabulous salary. So we're not short of money. My mum's one of the best tennis players at the club of which she's vice chairman. We've got a lovely house, one of the best in the village. We've got a nice house in Provence that we use for holidays, with swimming pool and tennis court and there are lots of restaurants nearby so we always dine out. I had a really good private education and I'm going up to Oxford in September. I've got a super girlfriend and my dad's just given me a car for my eighteenth birthday. It seems to me that things couldn't get much better for me or my family. So, how about explaining how being a Christian makes life better than that?"

Nick: "Thanks Ed. You don't make things easy do you? But, you know what? It's all about how you define "life". If life to you just means material success, your family has reached the pinnacle and I can't really add anything to that. But Jesus had a view on that: *"a man's life does not consist in the abundance of his possessions."* Knowing you as I do, I think you must already aware of that. I think you can see past material things.

Ed: "Yes, Nick, of course I can and I intend to use my skills in the future to play my part wherever the opportunity arises. But, apart from talking down material things, you haven't answered my question yet."

Nick: "Well, I am coming to that. However, I think it's best if I come at it from the end rather than the beginning. What I mean is there is "life" and there is "eternal life". "Life" comes to an end with death; "eternal life", as its name implies, goes on after death. In other words, your spirit lives on. The question is what quality of spiritual life awaits you. Believe it or not, that issue is decided here on earth during your "life".

Ed: "Now you've lost me with all that eternal life stuff. Why should I believe that and how does my life here affect my life "there"? "

Nick" The reason you should believe what I say is because it's written in the Bible. "

Ed: "But, Nick, there are commentators who think the Bible's a myth.

Nick: "Well, there have been many attempts over the years to prove that the Bible is a myth. And, certainly, such attempts have thrown up inconsistencies between the Gospels. However, these are basically of a minor nature. The Gospels are the written testimonies of four people, two of whom were actual disciples of Jesus and two of whom were closely associated with his disciples. What they wrote was what they heard and saw, either from Jesus or from his disciples. And like four witnesses to the scene of an accident, they may deviate somewhat from each others' stories but of one thing they are all sure. It happened.

It's the same with the Bible. It contains four accounts of the arrest, trial, punishment, crucifixion and resurrection of Jesus Christ. They happened. Anyway, don't take my word for it. There's a very good examination of the reliability of the Bible in a book written by Professor F F Bruce, called "The New Testament Documents, are they reliable?" or in Michael Penny's "The Bible: Myth or Message.""

WHY SHOULD I BECOME A CHRISTIAN? (2)

Ed: "OK. Assuming the reliability of the Bible, where do we go from there?"

Nick: "Well, it's in the Bible that we learn about Jesus and his teachings. He had a great deal to say about eternal life and it's not all good. In your life down here you make choices all the time: "What shall I wear?" "Where shall I go on holiday?" "What book shall

I read?"and so on. So it won't surprise you to learn that Jesus offers you a choice about where you will spend eternity. As he makes clear it's for you to decide whether it will be in heaven or in hell. And key to that decision is the question as to whether you have a relationship with God.

Ed: "Assuming I want to, how do I set about having that relationship?

Nick: "The first thing to say is that to have a relationship with God you need to be perfect or, as the Bible puts it, righteous. Why perfect? Because you need to accept that Jesus was the Son of God and that he died to set you free from sin. Now sin's an unpleasant word. It grates, doesn't it? We don't think of ourselves as sinners. No, we think of ourselves as people trying to do our best and that ought to be enough for God, if he's the right sort of chap. But if we're being honest, we've done or said things in our lives that we'd really rather we hadn't done or said – what the Bible calls sin. So, we're not perfect and there's the rub. From a spiritual point of view we can only have a relationship with God if we are as perfect as he is. There's no room for sin in heaven so we need to be perfect or, as the Bible puts it, wholly righteous. How do we achieve that? By accepting that Jesus' death cancelled out our sin and made us righteous.

That spiritual perfection does great things for us. For a start, it brings the Holy Trinity into our lives on earth. We get the benefit of God's love, the Holy Sprit's guidance and Jesus' offer that if you ask for anything in his name it will be granted provided, of course, that it fits with God's will for you."

Ed: "What you're saying is that a relationship with the Holy Trinity brings with it a wider dimension to my life?"

Nick: "Precisely. But, as I said at the beginning, it depends how you define life. Life for a Christian doesn't end with death on earth. It goes on beyond that. Jesus talked about those who put their faith in him as having eternal life. Can you imagine a life that goes on after our physical bodies are laid to rest? It's a spiritual life and we know it's just so wonderful it can't be fully described down here. That's where faith and hope come in. As a Christian I believe that Jesus rose from the dead to show us the way to eternal life. If I put my faith and hope in him I will follow him to that wonderful place we call heaven. Material success can't give you that! Nor, incidentally, can atheism!" Enjoy Oxford.

Ed: "Thanks, Nick. I will. You've given me something to think about whilst I'm up there."

THAT'S NOT YOU, IS IT?

Luke 16

Life on Earth

Dick: "Hello there, John. Is that a new Ferrari in the drive?"

John: "Come in, Dick. Yes, it's a cracker isn't it? I had a bumper bonus this year and that's the result. Six figures it cost. Worth every penny. I'm driving it down to Tuscany this summer, taking my son. Jan will have to come by air with Susanna and bring the luggage with them.

D: "You're doing really well. You bought that house in Tuscany last year, didn't you?"

J: "Oh yes. That was when my share options kicked in. Got it for a good price too."

D: "Do you let it out?"

J: "Good heavens, no. We can't have any Tom, Dick or Harry and their kids tramping through the place. Got some lovely antiques in there. Stay there while I get you a drink. The usual, I take it."

D: "Thanks John. What's that you're throwing away?"

J: "Oh that. It's one of those charity brochures. Red Cross, I think. You know what? Never touch them. Reply to one and they're on you like a pack of vultures. Anyway, it's not as though I don't do my bit. We always give a few quid to Christian Aid when they call. And I know for a fact that my wife gives some of my cast-offs to the local hospice. Anyway, if you'll excuse me, I've got some day-trading to do."

Life after Earth

J: " Dick! Can you hear me? Listen, I'm in terrible trouble over here. I'm burning in hell and I've got this constant thirst. I used to give you drinks, remember. Can you get me one? Water will do."

D: "I'm really sorry, John. I've checked with the authorities. They say there's nothing I can do for you. Apparently you had your chances on earth but didn't take them up. I'd come over and mop your brow if I could but I'm not allowed to cross over."

J: "But it's terrible over here and it's going to last forever. I just can't get my head round that. And the people here. They're just like me. We're all suffering. I can't get out of here but I'm sure someone from there could go back and warn everyone what they're in for if they're as selfish as I was.

D: "But John, they've already got Jesus in the Bible. If they don't believe him, they won't be convinced even if someone else rises from the dead. Goodbye John."

IN THE COURT OF FINAL JUDGMENT

I am really excited because this transmission comes to you today from the Court of Final Judgment. This is the highest court in the entire universe. There is no further right of appeal. I am the only reporter who has been given access.

I can tell you that the place is absolutely packed. There is no public gallery. There are no defence attorneys. Everyone in here is awaiting their turn at having their case heard, stating their defence and receiving their judgment. At the moment I am standing next to a middle-aged woman. She is holding, as is everyone else in here, a sheaf of papers on which I can see what looks like a long list.

Reporter: "Excuse me, madam. May I ask you what's happening?"

Woman: "Well, as you can see, this is a court room. As it happens, my case is the next one to be heard – and I'm not looking forward to it in the slightest."

R: "Why is that?"

W: "Look, you see this sheaf of papers I'm holding? It lists everything I have ever done, not done, said or thought in my life right from day one. There are things listed here that I had completely forgotten about. It runs to over thirty-four pages, covered on both sides. I haven't got a hope. If this goes to the Great Judge I'm lost. I mean, what hope is there for me when I have just seen a famous captain of industry condemned out of his own mouth? You can't lie in here, you know."

R: "What happened to him?"

W: "He made what I thought was a terrific defence. First of all, he had built up his company to become world class. Then he'd been head of a major charity. He'd chaired numerous bodies for the government. It seemed like there wasn't anything he hadn't done. I thought he'd sail through. Instead he was found guilty and condemned."

R: "I hadn't arrived at that point. Can you tell me why he was guilty when he seemed to have done so much good?"

W: "Well, once he'd been through the hugely impressive list of what he'd achieved the Great Judge only asked him one question: "Did you put your faith in my Son, Jesus Christ?" Do you know what he replied? "No, I didn't believe in him. In fact I used his name – and yours – as swearwords (Looks at list) fourteen thousand six hundred and thirty-five times.""

IN THE COURT OF FINAL JUDGMENT (2)

R: "So what happened to this captain of industry?"

W: "There are two ways out of the courtroom. One's marked "Followers of Jesus and Lovers of Righteousness". The other's marked "Others" So the captain of industry had to go through the door marked "Others". You've never seen such a hang dog look as I saw on his face. Oh, excuse me. My name's just been called. I'm on."

R: "Something truly astonishing has just happened. I am watching this woman going forward. I promise you, she can hardly walk she is trembling so much. In fact, she has just dropped her papers and collapsed, sobbing her heart out. At this point a man walks over to her, stoops down, picks up her papers for her, lifts her to her feet, comforts her and right there and then tears her list to shreds. Leaning on this man for support, she makes her way to the front. I can't hear what's being said but it looks as though the man is doing all the talking. Suddenly, she falls flat on her face. Well, she's up now and coming my way. I'm hoping to catch up with her before she leaves the courtroom. Here she comes. "Excuse me, madam. You seem a lot happier than when we were talking earlier?"

W: "Did you see that man that came forward to help me? Well, it was Jesus! You know what he said to me? "You're one of mine. Leave it all to me." It's true! It's true! I had faith but there was always a niggle of doubt."

R: "I'm sorry. I don't quite understand. What do you mean by "You had faith?"

W: "My life on earth was hard. I married a man who I soon realised never really loved me. He divorced me after four years and left me for someone else. There was very little joy in my life. Then, when my mother grew old there was no-one else to care for her so most of my time was spent looking after her. There came a time when I felt in absolute despair, with nothing to look forward to except getting old myself.

Then we got a new postman. He always had a cheerful word for me. I used to look forward to his arrival. It became one of the few highlights of my day. I asked him once why he seemed to be so happy. He told me it was because he had become a follower of Jesus. I didn't understand what he meant, so he invited me to come to his church."

IN THE COURT OF FINAL JUDGEMENT (3)

R: "Then what happened?"

W: "I went to the church and heard how Jesus can change your life and wipe out all your sins – all the things on my list. The minister invited anyone who wanted that change in their lives to come up at the end of the service. So I went, was prayed for and found out that Jesus really does change your life. I can't tell you how wonderful it was. My tears fell away and I felt a new person, able to face anything the world might throw at me. Even better, I fell in love with the postman. We married a year later."

R: " So how come you're here now? You were still in your earthly mid-life."

W: "That's the sad part. Three years after we married I was cycling to a prayer group when a truck swerved into my path and.....well, here I am."

R: " So can you tell me and my listeners what happened when your name was called out?"

W: "I still can't believe it! You saw the state I was in. I was scared to death to think that I was going to face judgment for all the things I had on my list. I could hardly walk. Then I made a complete fool of myself by dropping my papers and collapsing in tears. Then Jesus walks over, picks me and my papers up and tells me not to say a word.

When I get to the bench Jesus says something absolutely astonishing. He says, "This woman is one of my followers whom I have loved more than life itself. It will give me enormous pleasure to have her in my Kingdom. We have a party already arranged for her to celebrate her arrival. I have destroyed her list. She is free to enter my Kingdom." You know what I did next? I fell flat on my face. All I could say was "Thank you. Thank you. Thank you." I will never stop loving and praising Jesus for what he did."

R: "So what happens now?"

W: "I am going to go through the door marked "Followers of Jesus and Lovers of Righteousness." Goodbye and may God bless you as He has blessed me. It's all true Read the Bible, become a follower of Jesus and, when your time comes, follow me through that door."

R: "Well, listeners, there you have it. It's been the most amazing spectacle I have ever had to report on. I am leaving you now to find my Bible. Goodnight."

Lightning Source UK Ltd.
Milton Keynes UK
UKOW04f0001141213

223000UK00001B/1/P